Activating

Champions

Christopher V. Flett

Norsemen Books

Copyright Notice

Dedication

To my friend Jim "Jackhammer" Clark. He was a Champion not only of mine, but all business owners and professionals that were lucky enough to cross his path.

Table of Contents

Introduction
Getting to here

I started writing this book, sitting in an apartment in Tours, France, in the summer of 2019. I was finally walking the Camino Frances, after almost 20 years of talking about it, but never finding the time.

I had over 800 kms of walking time to consider what I wanted to say about Champions. From a strategic point of view, it is both the most straightforward and most sophisticated tool in my business development arsenal. Simple, in that it takes only minutes a week to manage; complex, in that you have to work through the process somewhat blind, feeling your way around until you fit the pieces together for your particular business model. The preparation is key to its success.

The hardest part of implementation is not rushing it. One has to complete each section before moving on to the next. If committed and patient, this strategy can revolutionize the way you originate business opportunities for your model. If rushed, it won't work, and the amount of time required to manage it down the road would be overwhelming.

After every book I write, I swear it will be my last. Why would someone put themselves through the process of putting ideas to paper while simultaneously loathing oneself for putting themselves in that predicament in the first place?

But for this book, it's a bit different. This model is one I love to teach clients and watch them implement. So I write this book for two main reasons:

The sheer number of questions I get from clients, colleagues, and audiences on how 'exactly' to create a bullet-proof system for finding, engaging, and managing Champions; and

1) I want to document my best practices should I get hit by a rogue scooter while travelling the world.

What is a Champion? We are going to dissect that entirely, but in its simplest definition:

"A Champion is an educated referral source for your business that not only finds you opportunities but also acts as a gatekeeper to keep time wasters away from you. They can qualify opportunities for you, and once they vet them, they present them to you selfishly."

Yes, selfishly. Champions want to bring you referrals because it is in their best interest to do so. Black magic, you say? Partially. But the foundation of any Champion strategy is mutually beneficial service to one another. More on this later.

What I love most about this business development strategy is that it can be incorporated into ANY business model, at any stage, for mutual welfare and benefit to all involved. This strategy isn't your daddy's referral network. This strategy is a full power business solution.

Since I'm confessing to you here, I've been sitting on the outline for this book for two years. Part of me doesn't want to be a writer or speaker in the way I was in previous years. It can get to be too much at times. But as I walked across France, the topic of Champions, and my desire to get as many people using it as possible, kept crawling into my thoughts. I realized that given my time constraints, the most effective way to get this information into the market is through book format. I struggled between trying to write the thesis of the entire idea, breaking down every little step, and not wanting this to take you more than a few hours to read.

I've worked this manuscript for the better part of 6 months now, trying to achieve an acceptable balance of this becoming your desk reference, and it not taking you too long to consume. I think I've accomplished that, but your use of these materials will tell the tale. Be like me and work this book. Dog-ear the pages, bookmark, mark up, highlight, and write all over this book. Make it a working tool. Should you destroy your copy of the book through use, simply send me your heavily used, devastated copy, and I will do what I can to expedite a replacement for you. But if you, like me, treasure the books that you have 'worked,' you may not give up that well-worked copy too quickly.

Aside from the value I know this book will bring you in developing a stable of Champions that produce constant and dependable opportunities for you, it will also accomplish something else. It will reconnect you with humans, in your business model, that may be in the peripheral but not engaged.

For everything that technology has done for us, it has robbed us of our connection with one another. One needs to only look in any restaurant, coffee shop, or airport to see how the most cherished relationship in our life is with the device in our hands. You don't have to give up your phone, but remember that business is done with humans, by humans, working together.

Finally, I have written this book with a more conversational tone than others you read. For those that have read my previous books, you'll note that I liberally use stories and examples to illustrate points. Here too. There might be some slang, colloquialisms, and language more resembling that you would hear from a friend. My style is universal, not polished. My spelling is British, even though I'm Canadian, and I work mostly in the United States. You are going to see added u's to your favorite words. It is the Queen's English, after all.

When I sat down to write this book, I imagined that I was talking to a client/friend (many of my clients are also friends). I believed that we had an afternoon together where I had the opportunity to share with them the inside working on Champions work. I focused on making sure the content is current, relevant, and applicable. Knowledge, without the ability to apply, is wasted.

Let's get to the work at hand. We need to forget everything we have learned about getting business. We are going to go back in time to take the best practices of our forefathers (and mothers) and reconnect to real business relationships to build better Champions and stronger business development activities for all involved.

The reward for your labors and those you engage with will be measurable and profitable bottom lines for your business models.

Quick Story: The Naysayer.

A few years back, one of my clients who oversees the national practice for a Financial Services Firm in the US asked me to connect with one of their established Portfolio Managers. He had a sizeable book, had been in the industry a long time, but had stalled on growth. I scheduled a call and, as I do with all 'first calls' after learning about his business, asked him the million-dollar question: "How much of your business comes from referrals?"

His response, "All of it."

He wasn't growing but was getting all his business from referrals. You can probably understand how this was confusing to me, so I asked for clarification.

He said that any new money coming in came from existing clients. They sold a home, got an inheritance, or some other transaction created cash for them, which funneled into their portfolio.

Seeing we were looking at this differently, I said to him, "Aside from new money coming in from existing clients, where do your referrals come from?"

His response, "We don't get referrals."

Let's put things in perspective. Here is a professional with over two decades of experience in the industry. He has a sizeable business and no active sources of referrals.

I asked him, "Do you ever make referrals?"

He replied, "All the time. There is one law firm in the building that we refer 7–8 clients a month to."

I asked him, "Do they send clients back to you?" He replied, "No. We have never received a referral from them."

I immediately saw the opportunity. This guy has all these people he feeds who don't feed him back. They either don't like him, don't know he's looking for accounts, or they don't know what to say about him, so say nothing. I decided to engage with this client to build out a Champion strategy for his practice.

The first session in, as we are getting things sorted, he tells me that he doesn't think it will work. I show him how and why it works, but he tells me that he wants to try something else. In good conscience, I can't go down that road with him, as I know that this strategy works and will work for him. So I conclude the engagement before we even get started. He's not happy as he wants to grow, but like many prospective clients, he thinks his way is better than ours so best for him to continue without us.

Fast forward six months. I'm speaking at the firm's National Conference in Boston. We have a bunch of clients at the conference, many of whom are at the top of the firm's producers' list. One of my clients invites me out to a wholesaler dinner, and as we enter the restaurant, we run into the Portfolio Manager I fired. I can tell by the look on his face, he's not happy we didn't engage with him and he says to me, "Well look who it is...Mr. Champion."

You don't know me, but I love uncomfortable situations. Like, really, really love them.

So I say to him, "Great to see you. How's business?"

He sneers and says, "It's about the same, but you already know that. Too bad you didn't have other tools to offer me rather than your Champion tool you were pushing. Champions don't work!"

So I ask him, "You've used the Champion strategy, and it didn't work?"

He replied, "Yes. I went out and told businesses we were referring business to, that they had to send us referrals or else we'd be cutting them off."

I smiled and said to him, "That's not the Champion Strategy; that's the Extortion Strategy."

He shook his head and walked off to the private dining room, where we were to have dinner. As luck would have it, I sat across from him at the dinner with one of my top clients sitting beside me. Our friend can't let it go, and midway through dinner, he wants to start up again about how 'Champions don't work.'

I've learned not to change people's minds when they make them up, so I smile. My client beside me pipes in (also enjoying uncomfortable situations) and says, "What do you mean 'Champions don't work'? Of course, they work. I build my business on that strategy."

The other wealth manager goes on to tell his tales about speaking with 'Champions' and telling them what they were going to do for him or else.

My client says, "well, you are approaching that all wrong, and if I were one of those people, I'd tell you to pound sand."

The other wealth manager says to my client, "Well, then you tell me how it works." My client smiles, as he loves the fact that he is telling a peer how my tool works when I'm sitting right there. And knowing that this wealth manager across from us is upset with me for not taking him on, he looks to rub salt in the wound.

He says, "Okay. Let me make this simple for you. I met Chris through the National Training Director at my old firm. This director was Chris' Champion and put him and Ghost CEO in front of 600 of our brokers. I wanted to get access to Chris, so I asked my director to get me a lunch meeting. He did. Chris and I decided to work together. When I moved to this firm, I introduced him to my new National Director. He met her. He began working with her. She's hired him as a coach, trainer, and keynote speaker for our firm. And she introduced him to you. I introduce him to clients; he introduces me to clients. When I meet someone I know he needs to meet, I make the introduction; when he meets someone I need to meet, he makes the introduction. And above all else, I protect advisors who are stuck in their ways, from wasting his time. The only mistake in this Champion strategy is his other Champion, who introduced the two of you, should have vetted you better. He's at this dinner because I want him to meet the wholesalers and the other brokers at the dinner. I'm giving him access to 20 qualified prospects. So yes. Champions do work if you work them."

That was the end of the conversation.

*Note: I've seen this gentleman 3-4x since that dinner and while he isn't angry anymore, he says to me each time I see him, "Chris, I just don't think Champions would work for my practice."

I just nod my head and smile. He's wrong, of course, but it's not my job to convince. Now those that practice the Champion strategy have a little saying when a Champion produces an opportunity. After the referral happens, we say, "But, Champions don't work." A slight nod to the people who are currently stuck with the wrong mindset and who I hope to get a copy of this book and see that it is easier than they may think it is.

Okay. Enough on this. Let's get into the meat of this book.

Chapter 1:

What Happened to Business Relationships?

To become proficient at building Champions in your business, you need to not look to what is 'new,' but instead, examine what 'old' is. Activating Champions isn't a new invention. It is a return to the fundamentals of developing relationships in business. For all that technology has advanced our ability to do more business, open up foreign markets, and sell twenty-four hours a day, it has come at a cost. The cost being the disintegration of relationships between provider and customer. Between strategic alliances. Between those that promote businesses and the businesses themselves. We have swapped out 'conversations' for 'chat.' And by doing so, we have sacrificed intimacy for convenience. This strategy works if you are selling widgets and are the cheapest.

But if you are selling a valuable service or product, the loss of intimacy, trust, and loyalty come at, in my opinion, too high a cost. We have more connections and are less connected.

But this hasn't always been the case. Before the technological revolutions, business used to be personal. Transactions centred on personal relationships that were developed, fostered, and managed with integrity, intention, and honesty. They were mutually beneficial, and everyone involved was satisfied with their benefit and their role if they were to be sustainable. Simply put, we cared about each other.

We used to be hyper-localized to our customers, sometimes as broad as a city and sometimes as small as a neighbourhood. Customers invested in businesses as their options were limited, and those businesses invested in their customer base, which was also limited. If you didn't take care of your customers, you would go out of business. If you didn't buy from your local butcher, barber, cobbler, or tailor, those businesses would be gone, and you'd find yourself without a provider. It was co-dependent in all the positive definitions of the term. You got your groceries from YOUR grocer. Your childhood barber would know when school pictures were and might wave you down as you walked by to remind you to come in. Your accountant could be YOUR accountant for life. We were loyal; we grew to know each other. We could forgive minor mistakes. We offered appreciation and acknowledgement to our business relationships. The longer we did business together, the stronger the bond. It worked for everyone because it had to.

But then the Internet emerged. The markets started to evolve. The world's cities began to grow. Consumers had more options than ever before. Customers began to be seen as disposable and started to feel that way. When they couldn't find a provider that would treat them the right way, they also moved away from focusing on relationship and loyalty, and made price and convenience the primary influence on what and how they bought.

As the adage suggests, 'it's time to get up from the table when Love ain't being served anymore.'

Markets (customers and providers) started to detach from each other, our businesses, and one another. This shifting market dynamic had a snowball effect on both consumers and providers. The consumer began seeing their providers focused more on getting as many clients as possible, rather than focused on client service. Customers started looking for the cheap/convenient options of those impersonal buying channels. The provider saw customers not being as loyal as they once were and now began to scramble to find new markets and ended up cutting prices and service levels to get their volume up. On both sides, it cycles down sadly.

Aside from technology giving consumers options and providers new channels to develop markets, another byproduct happened to dampen relations between business and consumer further. Technology created ways for us to 'communicate' without intimacy. We could send an email/text to someone and get a response from them without ever hearing their voice. We started disliking phone calls and instead wanted to engage or respond when 'convenient' for us. We became selfish with our time because work volume was up (we needed to do more business to make up for decreasing pricing). On both sides of the equation (consumer/business), we started to dislike each other, feeling we weren't getting the respect we deserved. Sadly, this is not just in business but everywhere now. You need only watch couples in restaurants, friends sitting in movie theatres, or people on planes, to see how engaged we are with our devices. We'd rather stare into a screen like a sheep than be engaged in conversation with one another. These devices are our new 'best friends', through which we can peer into the world through a virtual window. A sad, lonely, little window, where you can hide behind the blinds watching the world while simultaneously pretending you are 'not home' when someone knocks on the door, rings on the phone, or tries to engage with you in the real world.

What we have forgotten about business is that in its fundamental DNA... it is a team sport. Most companies need to be delivered and developed through the community.

When I think about successful business models in the real world, I don't think of Netflix or Amazon. While wildly successful, these companies are unicorns. Most businesses don't work this way, and to my point, these businesses cater to not having to engage in the human world. You can do your shopping from your laptop on Amazon, and rather than go out to the movies or rent a video (does anyone do that anymore? But I digress.

When I think of a 'sustainable' business model, built on relationships, trust, and intimacy, I think of an Amish barn raising.

If an Amish family wants to build a new barn, they can either:

- Try to do it themselves over a few weeks or months;

- Hire someone to do it for them and hope it works out all right and on budget; or

- Call all their neighbours, put on a picnic, and do the whole project in a day or two. I should add, you don't have to pay for the labour or the food as everyone openly and happily contributes to supporting the family.

The Amish build and develop as a community. They give freely, knowing that when they need help, they will have many hands offering support. Individual and community projects that might otherwise take weeks or months to complete are finished in a day or two. All with minimal financial resources. Activating Champions, in its purest form, is based on this communal model. You develop relationships, are clear with the needs of all involved, you offer value, and in turn, you receive opportunities, and business as a whole is easier for everyone involved. But you can't be selfish if you want it to work. You have to be clear about what you want to happen and precise about what you can offer. Both of which this book will help you to uncover.

To develop this type of community for your business, one that will help you 'raise your barn' (whatever that is for you), you need to make some slight, but challenging adjustments. We will go deeper into each of these, but here are the highlights to foreshadow what it takes to be successful with this strategy:

- Put down your phone and look people in the eyes.

- Know that technology plays a vital role in our productivity but can also undermine our relationships with clients, alliances, and Champions.

- We need to be clear with our goals and become 'curious' about the goals of others we do business with; people we align our business models with, people we serve, and others that are in our professional sphere of influence. Know who's 'building a barn' and what kind of barn they are constructing.

- For everyone you meet, think of what you can do for them, what they can do for you, what they can do for someone else you know, what someone else you know can do for them.

- Categorize your current and new business relationships into their spheres of influence, their superhero powers, and what type of business owner/professional they are, as though you are drafting a football team: type of player, the position they play, and what talents they bring to the table.

As you start to look at your professional world through this lens, you'll become increasingly surprised at how many people can make your business life more comfortable. They are great at areas that you struggle in; you are great in areas they struggle with. They know people you want to meet; you know people they wish to be connected to. They have answers to your questions. You have answers to their questions. This strategy is what crowdsourcing is in the real world.

When we implement this mindset and set of actions, the magic begins to happen almost immediately. All business grows in this environment, and all parties involved (industry, customers, and partners) benefit. You aren't the only one that wants this, or even craves this. All those heads pointed down at their phones need/want this too. They just don't know how to do it. You are going to learn how to do it, in this book, and then model the behaviour of coaching others how to do it as well. The multiplier effect happens as more people in your circle understand and practice these techniques.

But I'm already doing this!

Some of you will think you are doing a version of this already. You aren't. Those buzz words like 'centres of influence,' or 'referral sources' that we have all become so familiar with, are 95% of the time... tragic.

Referral sources and centres of influence are rarely activated properly, produce qualified prospects by luck, not by intention, and are mostly time wasters. There is a higher chance of not getting a return on your investment (time and money) than there is. On the odd occasion that you get something out of these relationships, it is just enough to trick you into thinking it works and so you continue wasting the resources mentioned above. Most professionals put these together like a ten-year-old builds a treehouse. Look around for things you could use, nail them together, and stand back, looking accomplished because you created something.

Let's examine the current strategies most people use to develop referrals:

1) Asking people for opportunities as a 'favour' and coming off as a 'leg humper.'

"Bob, can you think of three people that would like to protect their families with insurance?"

This tactic is hit or miss at best (mostly miss), and you will drive yourself crazy either 'humping legs' (wrong) or feeling frustrated that people aren't referring to you (duh..), which will not deliver revenue.

2) You are being The Good Samaritan hoping that your good deeds will lead to business.

"I sit on 17 boards, coach softball, donate blood. I'm sure those fellow boardmembers, parents, and community nurses will think of me if they need life insurance."

Waiting to get noticed is a terrible strategy.

3) Spend a tonne of money on marketing collateral and branding.

"I spent $20,000 on my brand, $10,000 on my website, and pay $3,000 monthly on billboards and bus benches. It's just a matter of time before I am busy with new customers. My branding consultant,

website developer, and advertising representative said I'm doing all the right things."

Unlikely unless you are selling a widget or something that doesn't require trust, intimacy, or loyalty from your market.

The examples above are hit or miss, uncomfortable to implement (so they won't be done well or consistently), and are the reason many get a bad taste in their mouth about business development. "Oh, I tried Business Development, and it didn't work." If you have said this, or are thinking this, you probably have been doing the wrong things, to attract the wrong people, with the wrong messaging, inconsistently. Sorry.

Unlike the treehouse builder, those that implement the Champion strategy are like a builder that has an architectural plan, properly engineered, and with all performance indicators in place. Math doesn't lie, and like building a house and developing

Champions, the magic is in the measurement and the management. It isn't emotional. It isn't a fluke. It's a set of steps and measurables to ensure you get on track and stay on track. Nothing to hide behind. No excuses. You execute it properly (which comes with practice), and you will never look back. The only regret you'll have is the years and money you put into 'centres of influence' that never really met their potential for you. But that's in the past, and we are looking forward.

Champions are to business building what GPS has been to flying. Rather than guessing where you are, you can pinpoint precisely where you are, where you want to be, and the path to get there.

Another positive outcome of the Champion technique is that it reconnects your existing relationships in a meaningful way and activates new contacts quickly. It taps into the fact that we are ALL selfish beings. We like to help others when it benefits us. The Amish farmer builds your barn because you are going to have to help him raise his. I know you may want to believe that people do things from the goodness of the heart, and maybe a small minority do, but most people do something because it serves them in some way. It isn't bad; it's human nature. So we play to that nature and look to develop win/win situations for those we engage within business. But before we can let this natural process happen, we have to let go of what we have been doing (three examples above) as it will cause us to stumble as we move forward.

Champion strategies require a blank page. We must go back to the fundamentals of human connection in the business context. We need to:

- Understand what Champions are.

- Understand how to find them, activate them, manage them, and feed them.

- Become a world–class Champion ourselves. To have exceptional Champions for our business, we must be outstanding Champions for their companies.

- Look up from our phones and into the eyes of each other.

- Look to connect with others truly, and they, in turn, will feel connected to us.

Champions who work together, win together. It becomes contagious.

As we close this section (and before we get to the homework), I want to remind you to leave behind the practices and beliefs that WILL sabotage this strategy:

- No wishing and waiting.

- No leg humping.

- No assuming brand and marketing collateral will do the work for you.

- No thinking you have already "done all this".

- No taking before giving.

- No proclaiming the importance of being a Champion without being one yourself.

- No betting on people's potential instead of their abilities.

Chapter Homework
(do this in a notebook)

1) Make a list of all the business development activities you've undertaken in the last six months. Rank them from most successful to least successful. For each one, consider how much time/money you invested and what your return on investment was (ROI) for each activity.

- How much did you enjoy each activity and which ones would you never like to do again?

- What was your top source for prospects/ leads /clients?

- Who was your most significant source of prospects/ leads/ clients?

- Who are you currently creating prospects/clients for? Any services or products that you are an unofficial ambassador/spokesperson/referral source? List them all.

2) Make a list of all the people that have referred a quality prospect to you in the last six months. Even if that prospect didn't close, still list the source.

Keep these lists moving forward as we will be using them in the implementation stage. After completing the homework, if you think of other people or things, come back and add to these lists.

Chapter 2:
The Power of Champions

Changing the way we think about getting business referrals may seem simple enough in theory, but in practice, it is much more difficult. It is much easier to train someone then to 're-train 'someone, as you have to overcome the habits and biases they bring to the situation. Some of you may want to keep doing what you have been doing and experiment with Champions periodically.

Approaching the strategy this way, will not work.

It's like saying you want to give up drinking but are just going to have a few beers each day until you don't. You want to keep one foot in the 'familiar 'and stick a toe in the 'new. 'Change is difficult, even if you are moving away from something that you know doesn't work. Give yourself time AND commit to having ten Champions in place within the next six months. Once you begin to see how Champions streamline your business development activities, this strategy will become your favourite.

But even so, you may start and say, "Chris...I don't think I'm going to find any Champions for my business."

This is false. You likely have 20–30 potential Champions already in your network that you haven't activated yet. They are waiting to be enabled. Let's get them suited and out there playing. You are going to have doubts. Hell, I did when I first started putting this strategy into practice, but as I built it (not having the benefit of this book), I began to get a glimpse of what could be possible, and I got excited. Reserve your judgement until the end of this book. Once you can start to visualize the picture, you can overcome any objections you have in your head (objections covered in Chapter 5), and you understand the recipe for how to get things going, then all I ask is for you to commit for 90 days. 12 short weeks. Three months. Activating Champions will change the way you do business for the rest of your career. I promise. If you don't see the magic, go back to the bus benches, leg humping, and sitting on boards, filled with unqualified prospects. That's the worst-case scenario friends, and sadly some of you are already there. Let's make things better.

* * * * *

Let's start setting our expectations, defining what a Champion is, and what role they will play in our business. This definition perfectly illustrates why these people are so crucial to the profitability and sustainability of your business model.

"Champions are an educated, unpaid sales force for your business that influences your niche market(s), and they expedite your connection with qualified prospects while keeping unqualified candidates away."

Let's unpack that definition a bit.

Champions are:

- Champions are educated referral sources.

- Champions are an unpaid sales force.

- Champions influence your niche market(s).

- Champions advance connections with qualified prospects.

- Champions keep unqualified prospects away.

In upcoming chapters, we will use these points as our 'yardstick 'when determining who will make an excellent Champion and who won't, as well as who is delivering as a good Champion and who isn't. If we can't measure it, we can't manage it, so everything to do with Champions will have measurement attached. Imagine, if you will, having ten well-educated salespeople with established relationships, all talking up your business, delivering you qualified prospects without you having to pay them.

Let's go a little deeper into each of the characteristics so that we fully understand the value they bring and the reason why this strategy is of utmost importance in your business model :

Champions are educated referral sources.

We have taken the time to articulate to our Champions what we do, why it matters, and who cares. We refer to these as the 'Three Questions'. During the process of education, we address any questions the Champion, or our niche markets, may have about our business model. Our business model must be crystal clear — nothing left up to interpretation. After knowing the solution we provide, we ensure our Champions know what type of prospects we are looking for, how to qualify them, and how to introduce us. We make it simple for Champions to showcase us to the right people, and protect us and our time from unqualified leads/opportunities.

Champions are an unpaid sales force.

These people are going to be producing value for us throughout their daily activities. From vetting prospects to making introductions, they are delivering all the opportunities of a seasoned sales rep without being on your payroll. And because they are external to your business and have a positive reputation with the people they are talking with, their endorsement and introduction hold even more weight than might come from a paid employee.

Champions influence your niche market(s).

Very important. We want Champions who already have respect and trust established in the niche markets you want to serve. They are a co-signer on our credibility to those we don't know yet. They are 'vouching 'for us.

People buy from people they like; people like people they trust; people trust people they know.

We are using the relationships, already established, between our Champions and their contacts. This reputation we are building expedites trust with our prospects.

Champions advance connections with qualified prospects.

What does a 'qualified' prospect mean? A qualified prospect for your business is someone who has:

1) a need for what you are offering; and

2) the means to pay for it.

Champions ask the prospect questions (that you have provided to them) to determine if a prospect has both means and need.

45% of the people they talk to will have means and not need (have money but don't need your solution);

45% will have need and not means (need your solution but don't have the money to pay for it).

The **10%** that remains (that have both need and means) get introduced to you for fit. These are our qualified prospects/leads.

By already being known and trusted by a prospect, your Champion plays a vital role in streamlining the prospecting process for you. Your Champion finds out what the prospect needs, describes how your solution could address their issue, and then they introduce the two of you. Their job is not to close the business for you (although sometimes they do), but instead to get you up to bat to have a conversation with the person, assuming they are a qualified prospect.

Champions keep unqualified prospects away.

As important as finding qualified prospects is, the Champion also acts as a gatekeeper to keep candidates that don't fit, from wasting your time.

Time wasters are the #1 problem I have with traditional referral sources. They end up giving you everyone when only 10% of that group is qualified. 90% of your time is blown on people that can't afford you or don't need you. This waste of time, through pointless conversations, is why people get a bad taste in their mouth for sales. They spend 90% of their time talking to the wrong people and not closing them. Then they tell themselves a story that they are bad at sales and do whatever they can to avoid it.

Champions give you back your time so you can focus on only talking to prospects that fundamentally fit your model. You have excellent meetings, your closing rate goes up, you fall in love with sales, and all is well in the world. You trade the small amount of time you use to train and manage your Champions for the enormous amount of time you have been wasting talking to the wrong prospects. It seems like a pretty good trade.

Not just for delivering qualified prospect introductions.

Champions create a more efficient path for us to talk to qualified prospects and give us back 90% of our previously wasted time to do other things. Awesome. But is that it? No.

Champions can play other roles in our business model. While sourcing qualified opportunities are significant (my favourite) and gatekeeping ill-fitting prospects a close second, there are other benefits that Champions can deliver. Here are some of the popular ones:

Establish credibility through association

Having a Champion who speaks well of you and your business model publicly adds a tonne of credibility to what you are doing. Even if they don't personally deliver you qualified prospects, your association with them can have a multiplying effect on the market's perception of you. Building off the reputation of a Champion can massively decrease the amount of time it takes to attract qualified prospects. If they know and respect your Champion, many of the prospect's barriers to buying come down immediately. Birds of a feather flock together. Association is powerful.

Market Intelligence – Insider Observations

Some Champions act as an early warning system on what's happening inside markets. Your Champion might notice trends in your industry that they make you aware of. This advanced warning offers you the ability to course correct.

In 2007, just before the financial meltdown, we had Champions both in the banking system and those serving that industry, bring to our attention trends they were observing in corporate training. These observations gave us time to change course from group training to one on one work. By getting the information ahead of time, we found ourselves well-positioned to benefit from the downturn. Many of our competitors/colleagues found out too late and went out of business. Had we not known, we may have taken severe damage like many.

Connectors

Champions will influence other prospective Champions/gatekeepers. While they may not directly introduce you to qualified prospects, they may introduce you to other Champions for your business. These potential Champions may be in a better position to connect you with qualified candidates or offer some of the other services we are listing here.

Champions delivering in this area tend to be people who collect professional connections and affiliations. The tell-tale sign for these types of Champions are people with vast LinkedIn networks or Rolodexes (does anyone even use a Rolodex anymore?). The average Champion you acquire in this practice will be worth at least one more Champion per year. Champions, who are suitable connectors to others, are probably worth four or more additional Champions per year. Champions are a renewable resource.

Sounding Board/Sober Second Thoughts

Some Champions become a trusted, confidential sounding board for our business ideas. They may be part 'bullsh*t 'meter 'and part 'fact-checker. '

These types of Champions let you carefully think through your ideas before executing them. They listen to your ideas from a different perspective and can offer a level of objectivity because they don't have a 'dog in the race. '

All of these additional Champion roles, aside from Qualified Prospect origination, are very important and valuable. You want to curate a team of Champions that reflects these different competencies so that you have both balance and bench strength on your side.

Many hands make light work.

In the next section we are going to start the process of doing our pre-work before we start engaging with our prospective Champions. As well, we are going to warm ourselves up to become an exceptional Champion for others.

Some heavy lifting is required, but the more work we do on our side, the less our Champions have to do on their side. When we make it easy for Champions, they activate quicker and produce measurable opportunities for us faster.

Chapter Homework

(do this in a notebook)

1) Make a list of who you currently have in your business circle that influences the market(s) you want to serve. Who would you like to play this

role? Make a list of your dream Champions doing this function.

2) Make a list of who you currently have in your business circle that is considered a leader in the industries you are serving and whose endorsement of your business model carries or would carry weight. Who would you like to play this role? Make a list of your dream Champions doing this function.

3) Make a list of who you currently have in your business circle that connects you with other people of influence. Who have they introduced you to in the last year? What has been the benefit to you for each introduction? Who would you like to play this role? Make a list of your dream Champions doing this function.

4) Make a list of who you know that has inside insight into your market(s) that could act as an early

warning system to let you know of market trends (good/bad) from which you can benefit. What information can they update you with? What can you ask them to watch for on your behalf? Who would you like to play this role? Make a list of your dream Champions doing this function.

5) Make a list of who you currently have in your network that can act (or acts presently) as a sounding board to your business development and client management ideas. This role should be someone who knows your market(s) intimately and can give you practical feedback on how things are likely to be received by your niche market(s). Who would you like to play this role? Make a list of your dream Champions doing this function.

You should have some useful lists once you have completed this homework.

Chapter 3:

Becoming easy to Champion

As with most things in life, preparation is vital. I've seen thousands of clients struggle with Champion development because they try to take shortcuts on the work required to be ready to 'receive 'Champions into their business model.

There are NO shortcuts.

You need to do this preparation process so that your unpaid, full-time sales force can do their job and develop opportunities for you. For every hour you put into this process ahead of time, you will get hundreds of hours back in benefit. Do not skimp or race through these steps. They are non-negotiable and necessary for getting the desired results. As we discussed in the first chapter, you have to leave what you have been doing behind and start fresh. Repurposing old things you used to do and trying to bolt them on to this new system will not work. Read that again. IT WILL NOT WORK. Follow this process correctly, as I have laid it out, and you'll be rewarded financially, professionally, and, most importantly, sustainably. Of this, I am sure.

We are going to refer to this phase as the 'pre-work.' We take this opportunity to get clear about what we are offering, which niche markets we are targeting and why.

Our Champions don't have to guess anything about our business model because we have clearly and concisely explained it.

We make it so simple, a 10 year-old could understand and will. We shoulder the burden of this work so Champions can focus on originating opportunities from the start.

Here's the list of work you will need to accomplish <u>before</u> you activate your first Champion.

Identify your three (3) niche markets.

Develop answers to the 'Three Questions" for each of your niche markets.

Determine what kinds of Champions you need and in what quantity.

Examine your list of prospective Champions, both those you currently have in your network and those you want to add from your 'wish list. 'This work goes back to our homework from the last chapter.

Get super active in your markets so that you can increase the value you offer your prospective Champions. Building a robust network makes you very attractive to Champions because your Champions benefit from that network.

Develop a clear set of business goals that you want to achieve over the next 12 months. These are goals you will articulate to all your Champions. By including them in your planning, they feel connected to contributing to the outcome. But they need to know what you are building, all with measurable goals.

You may have read this and thought... 'no big deal...I can finish this in a few hours. 'FALSE! This pre-work may take weeks to complete. The quality of your work here will directly relate to the production ability and outcomes of your Champions. We don't want to burn up a good Champion with a half-assed job on your part.

Remember, your Champions are unpaid. You need to make it easy for them to play their role, or they simply won't. The better prepared they feel, the more active they become. Unlike previous Chapters where I gave homework at the end, I'm going to provide you with homework to do in each part of this section before proceeding to the next step. Each section of this book builds upon the previous. Read a section and do the homework. Then move to the next section.

Don't jump ahead and don't take any shortcuts. It will be costly.

1. Developing three niche markets

Developing three niche markets is one of the fundamental tools of the Ghost CEO™ and one we take very seriously. All business models need to have three (3) niche markets they are developing at any given time. Two is too few (you don't have enough variety); four is too many (your resources will be spread too thin to penetrate effectively).

We are looking to target three different and independent markets from which to find and close clients and opportunities. Diversifying your niche markets is key to protecting yourself against 99% of market corrections that may happen. It's like having a diversified stock portfolio. As we wade into the niche markets, let's calibrate the definition, so we are on the same page.

> A niche market is a group of prospective clients that act alike, look alike, and have many similar (if not exact) characteristics and drivers.

For those that read 'Market Shark – How to Be a Big Fish in a Small Pond '(2014), we dive deeper into how to define these markets, but we are looking for three characteristics when identifying the right niche markets for clients:

1) It has to be big enough that you don't exhaust the prospect pool. The niche has to continue to repopulate itself, so your development in it will not run out at some point.

2) It has to be small enough that you can become the 'go–to 'person for that niche market.

3) You have to be able to clearly define your niche markets to others, so they understand what it is and how to identify it. You also need to know the problem that you solve for these markets.

The challenge most professionals face is that they don't adequately define their prospective customer base. When asked who their 'ideal 'or 'target 'market is, they say, 'well... anyone really'. This answer is lazy and passes the responsibility onto the market (or prospective Champions) to figure out rather than making it easy for the general public (and potential Champions to know where you fit and with whom). If your target customer base is 'everyone, 'then that means 'no one. 'Imagine looking for a date, and your matchmaker says:

"What kind of person are you interested in?"

And you reply,

"Anyone, as long as they have a heartbeat."

This answer makes it pretty hard for your matchmaker to do an excellent job in finding you the 'right 'person. Yes, they can throw a bunch of options at you, but 99.9% likely won't fit, and you'll be wasting both your time.

If you are expecting your Champions to source prospective clients out of too big a pool, this added effort will cause them to lose interest in helping you, and they won't. It's a missed opportunity for you to have someone sourcing the right people because you couldn't be bothered to complete the preparation required to engage them.

It is important to note that this is one of the steps professionals get most uncomfortable doing. They don't want to be specific for fear of losing out on opportunities. This fear comes from them not knowing how to source qualified leads and thus being scared that something might get missed. Have the courage to become known in three markets, and the market and Champions will reward you for your focus.

The objection that always comes up from our clients (99% of the time) is:

"What if I define three markets, and I miss out on other markets who don't think I service them?"

This scenario will not happen. Those that are not part of your market catchment will ask you if you might consider working with them or if you know someone who will. If it is someone you can serve, you will; if it isn't, you can refer it out, thus being a Champion for both the prospect AND the business you are referring to. It works that easily. To have good Champions, you need to be a great Champion. Being known to specifically service markets will increase your prospect pool, not decrease it. People will start to see you as 'that person who provides a product or service 'for a particular type of client.

Let me illustrate the point using a scenario you should be familiar with.

You have lots of friends. They have varying interests. But imagine you have one friend who is crazy about Ford Mustangs. She has posters. She has Christmas ornaments. She owns a '68 fastback. She goes to rallies, and her favourite movie is "Gone in 60 Seconds" because of 'Eleanor'.

She is Mustang Crazy. You are out and about shopping, and you come across a new store that is all Classic Mustangs. Sweaters, mousepads, books, iPhone cases, and all other types of branded items.

You are thinking of all the people in your life. Which one person do you reach out to let them know that there is a Mustang shop they need to visit? Would it be that friend that has educated you on their particular and unique interest? Had they only told you that they like cars, you may not have gone out of your way to let them know about this shop. But because they clearly defined their unique interest, you are compelled to let them know because of how grateful you know they will be.

This clarity of market interest and positioning is how the market and Champions work in doling out referrals or identifying opportunities. When they know what a solution is and for whom, they look to match the person with the problem with a suitable solution. It makes them feel good and scores them points with the person with the problem.

The more exact you can be with the markets you serve, the more effective your Champions can be with matchmaking you and qualified prospects. The next question we need to ask ourselves is, how focused do we need to be with our niche market targeting?

Think back to the three characteristics we want in our niche markets:

1) Big enough that we don't run out of prospects;

2) Small enough for us to become the 'go-to person';

3) We need to clearly understand the market and the problem(s) they have, to which we have an obvious solution(s).

Let's bring it into focus by using lawyers as an example. Lawyers are not a niche market. It is too broad. But here are examples of niche markets:

1) <u>Female Lawyers in Seattle</u> (geographic and gender-based) are a niche market.

2) <u>Lawyers specializing in mergers and acquisitions</u> in Vancouver and Toronto are a niche market.

3) <u>Lawyers who attended UCLA</u> in the last ten years are a niche market.

4) <u>Hispanic lawyers </u>that are senior partners at East Coast law firms are a niche market.

All are definable, visible, and all are markets that replenish themselves. The niche markets you are targeting need to be identifiable and unique. You want to be able to clearly explain what niche markets you work with, where they practice geographically, and how to best engage these markets (watering holes, communications platforms, and other venues.)

When you figure out who you are targeting, you are one step closer to activating your Champions (foot soldiers) to go into these markets, with the right information, and return to you with opportunities and introductions.

Chapter Homework

(do this in a notebook)

Make a list of three markets you want to focus on with Champions. You aren't saying 'no ' to other clients, but for your Champions, you are focusing on these three. Run the 'niche test 'on each market you've selected:

- Is it big enough that you won't run out of prospects?

- Is it small enough for your presence to have an impact?

- Can you clearly define/identify it in one sentence?

If you are having problems identifying niche markets, choose your three favourite clients.

Profile them. What makes them unique? What groups are they associated?

2. Developing answers to the 'Three Questions" for each niche market.

Once you have identified the three niche markets you are targeting and activating Champions in, you then need to determine the messaging for these markets so your Champions can deliver adequately and seamlessly on your behalf. To accomplish this, we need to answer the following three questions:

1) What do I do?

2) Why does it matter?

3) Who cares?

If you want to nerd out on the fundamentals of the Three Questions, a more in-depth explanation can be found in Market Shark (2014), but again, for our purposes, here is the information that these questions convey about your business.

What I do? This question identifies the solution that you bring to the table for the market you are talking to (one of your three niches).

Why does it matter? Address the pain points or advantages of your solution to the benefit of the niche market(s) you serve.

Who cares? The specific niche market that will likely have the means and the need for what you do – what we would consider a qualified prospect.

There are some basic rules on how we answer these questions to ensure they are 'Champion Ready.' They have to fulfill the following requirements to ensure they are universally "useable."

- Answers can be no more than one sentence long (and not a run-on sentence).

- Answers customised to the niche market you are targeting so that specific client group, hearing your response, says 'Hey.. they are talking about me!"

- Answers must be easily repeatable by others (simple enough to be recited by a 10-year-old).

This task is where the hard work starts to feel a bit harder. Stick with it! We need to develop answers as close to perfect as possible so that when our Champions deliver them on our behalf (inside our niche markets), it catches the attention of the market we are targeting. Thus we have created visibility (they know we exist) and credibility (they start to believe we are good at what we do). This hard work all leads to profitability, and we haven't even talked to them yet in person. Bus benches and leg humping be damned.

Answering the questions is going to be a challenging exercise for you, and it's your business. Imagine how difficult it would be for a Champion to try to come up with an answer for you.

There are only three reasons people aren't referring you to the right prospects:

1) They don't know you are looking for new clients (because you haven't told them), or they don't know what types of clients you are targeting.

2) They think you are incompetent or an A**hole.

3) They don't know what to say about you, so they don't say anything for fear of not representing you well (90% the time, this is the issue). You find this out when you activate a current contact into a Champion, and they start producing opportunities for you. It wasn't that they couldn't support you,

you just hadn't prepared them properly. Your fault, not theirs, but we can fix this.

Numbers 1 & 3 we can fix by activating your Champions and give them the right answers to repeat and pointing them in the right direction.

If Number 2 is the reason they aren't referring you qualified leads and opportunities, you need to figure out why your contacts don't fancy you that much. Ask a friend to give you blunt feedback. If I were your friend, I'd do this.

The measurable we are looking for:

Once you have the answers to your three questions developed, you then feed them to your Champions and watch to see what the response is. The first 'win 'for you is getting your Champions to say the right thing. The second 'win 'for you is having someone in your niche market want to find out more.

Every Champion that can answer your questions correctly multiplies your effectiveness in the market. 10 Champions are 10x more capable than you speaking to people on your own.

Further, when you do this work to prepare to empower your Champions to act on your behalf, two byproducts emerge.

Firstly, you become more clear about what you do, which makes it easier to attract prospects because you better articulate what solution(s) you provide and for whom.

Secondly, new Champions emerge who were not previously on your radar screen because they understand what you do and may know people looking for that solution.

Before giving you the homework in this section, let's do an exercise where we work through the three questions. Remember, these will never be perfect (perfection is unattainable), but they will be close. The closer we get to our final answers, the more qualified prospects you get. So we develop our responses, activate our Champions, measure the results, and refine (or re-engineer). This work is ongoing as your markets are always evolving. Your answers will develop, as well. You will start to use your answers when they are 'pretty good 'and stop messing with them when prospects get excited by the answers. Don't change your answers when they are working. Once they are working, let them work. Once they stop being productive, re-engineer them.

You'll note that the answers we come up with aren't perfect, BUT will be 100x better than anything anyone else is using. That's where we get the immediate advantage and where we can activate Champions who clearly understand what we do, why the solution matters, and who should know about it.

Example:

Sarah is an accountant for an established firm in Portland. She knows she needs to bring in more business for the firm but is unsure how. She is developing Champions as part of her strategy to meet more prospects, present more solutions, and close more business.

Here is an example of how Sarah would answer the questions in the beginning, before refining her answers:

What do I do?
I'm an Accountant.

Why does it matter?
People need Accountants.

Who cares?
Anyone who is in the market for an Accountant.

Sarah is a great accountant, but her answers are boring and beige. It is what we would all expect her to say. So she falls back into the white noise of the market, forever to be forgotten as 'just another accountant.'

After doing this work with clients since 1999, the example above is the standard version of answers I hear, regardless of industry. They are practical, intentional, and sadly look a lot alike. They are unremarkable, even though with a slight scratch of the surface, we start to see the 'shine 'that would catch the market's attention. We just need to uncover and do a little polishing. A bit of elbow grease, but well worth the effort.

Let's say that Sarah decides she wants to focus on technology companies in Portland that are quick growing, undertaking R&D (research and development) activities, and are hyper mindful (and sensitive) of their burn rate (how quickly their company spends money).

If Sarah gets a chance to pitch to these types of technology companies (highly unlikely), without doing the pre-work, she is going to sound like every other accounting firm, and the only thing she is going to compete on is the price.

But if she takes the time to tailor her message to this niche market, not only will she grab their attention, but she will likely secure the work, even if she is more expensive than the competition. All because they will see her as 'specialising 'in their particular niche market (think Mustang Store).

Sarah, inspired to stand out and maximize the opportunities to capture this niche market's attention, starts re-working her answers. After many hours thinking, drafting, scrapping, and polishing, her Three

Questions now sound like this:

What do I do?

I'm an Accountant that works with fast growing technology firms to maximize their R&D credits and minimize their tax responsibilities.

Why does it matter?

Fast-growing technology companies need to preserve cash flow to expand their markets, company, and bottom line.

Who cares?

Technology companies that want an accountant who knows how to have them keep as much of their capital as possible and get all the tax credits and rebates afforded to them through their activities.

*This set of answers is far from perfect but is ready to feed to Sarah's Champions. You can start to see how intentionally developing this information can reap tremendous results. If there are twelve accountants lined up side by side for a Portland tech company to interview, eleven of those accountants will answer the same. Sarah will use the set of answers she took the time to craft, customized for technology companies.

If you were that CFO of that tech company, which accountant would get your attention? One of the eleven accountants that all sound the same or the accountant that specializes in your exact situation?

A prospect will respond to a solution that most resembles their issues. Invest the time; reap the rewards.

Let's change the lens to a prospective Champion/strategic alliance. Imagine you are a service provider that supports fast-growing technology companies in Portland (let's say a commercial realtor), and you meet Sarah at a networking event and find out that she specializes in fast-growing technology companies that undertake R&D activities. She is going to immediately capture your attention because she specializes in a market that you also target. You are going to file her information away in your head in case one of your commercial clients needs a great accountant. Later on in the month, one of your tech clients is complaining to you about how much their R&D and taxes are costing them. The first thing that might pop into your mind is:

"Client has the wrong accountant, needs someone who understands how to minimize taxes and capture tax credits. I must introduce them to Sarah."

You want to look like a hero to your clients by giving them a 'customized' solution to their unique problem. You just "happen to have" someone to introduce to them. This opportunity is the time for you to look like a hero to them.

Here's what that conversation would look like if you were in visiting with the client, and they were venting to you about the stresses of tax and operational overhead.

The client of Commercial Realtor (Prospect of Accountant):

> *"The IRS is killing us with a tax bill, and we are spending all our money on R&D, which is running us into cash shortfalls. It's such a pain in the butt and stressful."*

Commercial Realtor (Champion of the Accountant):

> *"Hey. I know an accountant that specializes in working with tech companies in minimizing their tax responsibilities and accessing R&D credits from the government. Would you like*

me to introduce you to her? Could certainly help with your cash flow and stress issues.”

Prospect:

“Yes, please!”

In this situation, Sarah has made it easy for her Champion (Commercial Realtor) to bring her a qualified prospect because she has outlined the type of client she serves, the solution she provides, and the benefit to the client. The Champion didn't have to figure it out any of this on their own. They were fed the information in a way that was easy to share with others.

This type of outcome is why we do the pre-work. So our Champions don't have to. Had Sarah just said she was an accountant, she would look no different from the tech company's existing accountant and wouldn't be noteworthy for the Commercial

Realtor to bring up in conversation after hearing about the client's problem.

Chapter Homework

(do this in a notebook)

For each of your three niche markets, draft your answers to the Three Questions (three sets of responses in total)

Run this test on each of your answers:

- Is it one sentence long and not a run-on?

- Is it customized to be memorable to the target niche?

- Is it repeatable by a 10-year-old?

- Find a 10-year-old. Tell them what you do, why it matters, and who cares. Ask them to describe back to you what you do.

3. Determining what kinds of Champions you need and in what quantity

After identifying your three niche markets and answering the three questions for each, it's time to start sourcing and considering Champions. Within each niche market, we want to look at who we already know that could be a Champion and with whom we need to develop relationships. There are many people with Champion potential. If they can't produce for you, you disqualify them from being your Champion. We do not go after (or keep chasing) Champions that have potential but don't deliver.

We focus on ability, not potential.

Alternatively, there might be people you have written off that simply didn't have the right information to represent you accurately. It's time to let everyone have a new chance at making it on your Champion list. You will examine each person through this new lens and updated information, and then decide on if they can be a Champion for you and you for them.

Because there are different Champion roles, you need to fill in each niche, start by identifying ten prospective Champions for each market as a way to get the ball rolling. Many of these people will not progress to Champion activation. We need to go through the motions to dial in our strategy. Even when fully dialled in, we will measure and manage their monthly performance on our behalf (and our activities on their behalf) to ensure our list of Champions is the best it can be.

Those that don't produce (or we can't produce for) get dropped. Those that are stars get even more of our attention. Just like any successful sports team, we are always on the lookout for the next best player and figuring out how to draft them onto our team.

We take care of the stars and drop the boat anchors.

In each of your niches, I want you to have:

- Six Champions that can refer you business;

- Two that are your market experts on what is happening; and

- Two that act as your sounding boards.

We will start there, hoping we get three per niche market, to begin with, and accepting that seven will fail to meet expectations and not activate or produce. It's a numbers game. We don't become emotionally tied to who is on the boat; we are committed to getting results.

Chapter Homework

(do this in a notebook)

1) We need <u>ten prospective Champions per niche</u> market (30 in total). Get out a piece of paper and split it into three columns with the name of each niche at the top of each column. Brainstorm people you already know that could be a Champion for you in each of your niche markets. Make as extensive a list as you can. We can always edit later. Do a full brain dump over anyone and everyone in your sphere. An excellent place to start is going through your social media networks to get your wheels turning. Facebook and LinkedIn are my favourites.

2) After you have exhausted your existing list of contacts, start adding people you have heard

of, know of, or whom you have had a previous encounter. These are people you are going to spend a little more time looking at once you have done your initial sweep and processed existing contacts.

3) Ask your contacts who they know who are leaders in your markets. This action is the simplest way to build your list and the one most overlooked — crowdsource the work when possible.

This extensive and expanding list of existing and potential contacts becomes your 'shopping list 'for the sake of this exercise. You need to know who you are targeting before you can come up with the strategy of how to engage them (figuring out what their selfish reason will be to Champion you). In the next chapter, you will see the step by step process we go through to 'test 'the viability of a prospective Champions before engaging — no point investing time and resources if they don't meet our requirements on paper first.

REMEMBER: This process can feel overwhelming when you start. Your mind starts racing. You start mentally struggling with whom to talk to. Take a big breath. Like riding a bike, it is hard until it isn't. We have time to develop this and want to take that time to understand each step thoroughly. Time is not your enemy; impatience is.

You likely have a tonne of Champions already in your life that you simply haven't activated yet or appropriately activated. Don't make this harder than it needs to be and don't rush it. We aren't going to talk to everyone; we are going to approach this process strategically and sequentially. Don't forget that this is a new skill for you and one that you will use throughout the rest of your career. Practice the technique slowly and intentionally. The stronger the foundation you develop, the stronger this technique will be for you in the short and long term. What I've noticed in working with clients in implementing this strategy since 1999, is that the slower and steadier they take the process of implementing a Champion Strategy, the better the short and long term results are.

4. Get more active in the 'watering holes 'of your niche markets so that you can increase your value to your prospective Champions

Time to get a bit more social than you might typically be. Act like you are running for political office. Shake many hands; kiss many babies.

If you are an introvert and you hate this stuff, find selective ways to get out and engage in a way that is more comfortable for you. Maybe going to smaller events, or with someone you already know. Or whatever you need to do to feel both comfortable and meet new people.

If you are an extrovert that can't help but talk with everyone, we are going to temper that a bit so that your activities are measurable and sustainable, and not rushed (sounding like a broken record yet?).

Introverts tend to miss opportunities with Champions.

Extraverts tend to mismanage opportunities with Champions.

Regardless of which type of personality you most identify with, we do all of this in 'baby steps. 'We want to add to our professional network and contacts regularly and intentionally. This practice is most efficient by visiting and engaging the 'watering holes ' that your niche markets frequent. It offers you the most significant return for the time investment and, aside from connecting you with new people, can provide vital market information and perspective.

*A Watering Hole is slang for a place where your niche markets hang out. It could be a monthly meet up, an association meeting, conference, trade show, or the like.

Time is the resource we all struggle with and is of finite supply. We want to make sure our time investments make sense. The first step is to decide which "watering holes" are best for each of your niche markets. Before we can assess the watering hole, we need to identify them. The best way to find out where watering holes are is to ask one of your prospective Champions, who know the lay of the land for that particular niche. They can give their opinion on which watering holes are worthwhile and which ones are a waste of time and money. Remember that everyone will have a different experience at a watering hole.

What was useless for one person might be fruitful for another. Identify all the opportunities and then go yourself, if possible, and see if it offers you value in building your network and connections.

Back when I first wrote, 'What Men Don't Tell Women About Business – Opening Up the Heavily Guarded Alpha Male Playbook '(Wiley, 2007), I toured the female professional watering holes across North America. I spoke to or networked at various chapters of:

- Commercial Real Estate Women

- Women Lawyers Bar Associations

- National Association of Professional Business Women

- American Society of Women Accountants

- Professional Mortgage Brokers Association

- Women Business Owners

- Women Presidents Organization

- And dozens of others.

Some groups would be excellent in some cities, terrible in others. It depended on the location, the group, and the mandate of that group, I went to groups others told me to avoid, and they were exceptional. I went to ones that others said were amazing and got skunked (no opportunities). But I remained curious and still do. I want you to become curious too. When you become curious, you to the right mindset for opportunities, I should add that there were variances, even within organizations. I may visit one chapter of a national organisation in LA, and it was terrible; visit a different chapter in Coral Gables, and it was awesome. Every event got the most curious and interested version of myself.

Chapter Homework

(do this in a notebook)

1) Make a list of prospective watering holes for each of your niche markets. Remember to ask your contacts within those niches where they go and their option of those events/activities.

For each watering hole, track when they meet, if the group has speakers, if they have a networking component, and if they are open to the public or if you have to be a member.

2) Reach out to the people responsible for planning and find out more about their events.

3) If applicable, schedule to go to an event and check it out for yourself. Always try to be curious and open to all potential opportunities.

4) Take a few minutes directly after each event, and document what was noteworthy, what wasn't, the quality of people attending, any important connections you made, and for those connections that were relevant, follow up with a handwritten note and an invitation to connect.

Remember watering holes will connect you deeper with prospective clients, put you in front of potential Champions, and introduce you to connections you may be able to leverage down the road.

5. Have a clear set of business goals that you want to achieve in the next 12 months. These are goals you will articulate to all of your Champions moving forward.

Whenever applying a strategy within business development, make sure it is attached to a measurable goal or goals that you have set.

If you can't measure it, you can't manage it.

You need to know, at all times, if you are moving towards or away from your intended outcome. As you implement the Champion Strategy, here are the main KPIs we use for measuring our activities. As well, here is a set of goals for you to perform in the next 12 months. The clock starts when you activate your first Champion. Think of it as a game that makes you money.

Key Performance Indicators:

- Number of prospective Champions identified (month/quarter/year)

- Number of potential Champion conversations held (month/quarter/year)

- Number of Champions activated (month/quarter/year)

- Number of total prospects received from Champions (month/quarter/year)

- Number of qualified protects received from Champions (month/quarter/year)

- Number of touch points you did outbound to your Champions (month)

- Champion turn (how long people stayed active Champions of yours – they actively created opportunities or provided measurable value to you and your business model).

Goals for the Champion Strategy
(12-month period):

1) Have the Champion conversation with 40 people.

2) Develop ten active Champions (that have produced opportunities for you)

3) Receive at least 60 quality introductions from your Champions

4) Obtain at least 40 qualified prospects from your Champions

5) Close at least 20 new clients/opportunities from your Champions

6) Deliver monthly value to each of your active Champions (more on how to do this later in Chapter 8).

You can shift these goals accordingly, but unless you have a good reason, use the ones I've laid out here. It will work for 95% of people reading this book. Let me unpack how I came to the goals here and why they make sense for you to incorporate.

Have the Champion conversation with 40 people.

About 25% of the people you target as Champions will be interested in becoming an active Champion. You are going to have some Super Introverts in there. There will be others that don't want the stress of having to deliver. Lots that you talk to are business hobbyists and not serious business people (sad but true). Accept that we are targeting a 25% closing rate. That means 75% of those you target won't fit.

As you have more of these Champion conversations, you'll start to develop measurables that will let you know in less time, if someone has the 'right stuff 'to become one of your Champions and you one of theirs. Having a success rate of 25% may not be appealing to you, but trust me, it's perfect.

Developing ten active Champions.

Ten is a manageable number for you to handle as you implement this strategy. There is nothing worse than activating a quality Champion, only to mismanage the relationship, due to inexperience, and lose them. In the beginning, I did this many times myself because I got busy, distracted, (fill in the excuse), only to kick myself later because I lost that activated salesperson that was producing opportunities for me.

What's ironic is that Champions get you busy with work and with them producing for you, it becomes challenging to keep up with them and ensure you are 'showing them the love. 'Champions are as <u>crucial</u> as clients from a business development perspective. A client may be worth whatever revenue you generate from them; a Champion is worth, on average, 12 clients a year. The best is when clients become Champions. More on this later.

Having ten active Champions is manageable, no matter how busy you are. It's just enough to let you cut your teeth on how to maintain and support these essential relationships. Once you have ten active Champions, you will see (on average) one qualified opportunity per month, per Champion. Along with managing the connection with your Champions, you also need to handle the opportunities they create in your Sales Funnel.

Champions don't like giving you opportunities that you mishandle. It makes them look bad, and if you drop the ball, they stop doing what you want them to do. So make sure that you are ready to handle the opportunities, connections, and business if you are activating Champions.

After you successfully manage ten Champions for six months, you will then increase the size of your Champion stable to 25. Don't get sketched out. You are already thinking ten seems challenging, and now I'm talking over double that. Relax. There is a process.

In business development, we are always looking for clients. We are also always on the hunt for Champions. You will find the additional fifteen Champions relatively easy once you have the first ten. Each of those current ten Champions will introduce you to another person like them. Assuming, of course, you are managing them properly, handling opportunities well, and making them look good. If each Champion introduces you to just one person like them over the six months, you are up to 20 Champions. And if you are visiting watering holes (to increase your network and value to your Champions and clients), you will come across five more. That's twenty-five. When I think of some of my top

Champions over the last five years, each of them has introduced me to at least 50–100 top clients and 50–100 top Champions.

Once we hit 25 Champions that are activated and producing, we sit there for another six to twelve months. You need to ensure you are managing the bigger group properly. Throughout this time, you will be adding Champions, dropping Champions, but overall have a pretty steady stable of killers working on your behalf (and you on theirs).

You manage your Champions at this level for between 12 and 18 months until you become comfortable with it. This is the point in development where things get dangerous. You might start making mistakes on how you are engaging your Champions. You may begin to take them for granted. You might not think that any one Champion is that important. These can all tilt your activities and drop you back to zero, so be careful. Champions at this stage are going to take between 1-2 hours of your time to manage weekly. However, for that 1-2 hours of investment, you are getting 25 unpaid sales people in the market sourcing opportunities and contacts for you — an enormous return on investment.

At the 18-month mark, assuming you are doing everything well (handling opportunities well, communicating well with Champions, championing your Champions, etc.), you look to double your stable. How? You will do what you did to get yourself to 25. Each of your 25 Champions will introduce you to one more person like them. 25 becomes 50. That's assuming you aren't drafting Champions as you meet them on your own.

<u>Caution!</u>
Do not surpass 50 active Champions.

At 50 Champions, you'll need to set aside about 2 hours a week to manage these critical relationships. You excel at managing your Champions. When you are out and about, you find opportunities and connections for multiple Champions that you can deliver to them. In Chapter 6, we will get deep into how you become the model Champion for your network. But why do I want you to limit the stable to 50 Champions? Two reasons:

1) You want your Champions to feel like a member of an exclusive group.

2) More than 50 Champions are hard to track and take care of.

Even if you find yourself spending more than two hours a week caring for your Champions, it's a good investment. Properly activated Champions can replace about 85% of your business development activities. It's pretty exciting to leverage the power of your educated fans and streamline your process of filling your Sales Funnel with qualified prospects.

Though it is fun to think about what this can become in the future, we need to focus on the first step. If we don't execute that well, the rest is moot. There are no shortcuts. Perform it slowly and with intention. Follow the timeline set out here. When you get it right the first time, you end up way ahead instead of having to repeat things because you rushed.

First six months	find first 10 Champions
6–12 months	manage 10 Champions
12–18 months	25 Champions
>18 months	50 Champions

Receiving 60 quality introductions from your Champions.

These introductions will be to both prospective clients and prospective Champions. 60 is very reasonable considering that it will take you a few months to get everything sorted, Champions activated, and making magic happen.

A fully activated Champion will produce one qualified prospect or opportunity per month. As they learn how to be a great Champion, you decrease your expectation of them to just one 'quality 'introduction, every other month.

That's six per year per Champion x ten Champions. Some of your Champions might come hard and fast right out of the gate and give you two in a month; others might generate one every quarter. We are looking for an average of one per Champion every other month.

Receive 40 qualified prospects.

Continuing with the previous point, receiving 40 qualified prospects, will validate and cement the immense importance of this strategy for you and your business model. Not all of these opportunities are going to become new revenue for you. However, getting "up to bat" 40 times, because you've educated a third party to speak on your behalf, is intoxicating.

As you drink from that cup, you will become even more encouraged to make it part of your daily practice. And you will understand why some Champions are fantastic, while others aren't. You will start to 'scout 'talent like never before. It will be exciting, you'll love it, and you'll be thankful you wrestled with all the hard pre-work like your niche market identification and answering the three questions.

Close at least 20 opportunities from your Champions.

This part is where the 'rubber meets the road' on this strategy. You are making money (yes, actual money) from the implementation of this strategy.

At this point, about 50% of the opportunities your Champions create, will close for you because they have already been pre-qualified and pre-closed by your Champions. Prospects, at this stage, are yours to lose.

If your closing process is sharp and you can back up the answers to your three questions, you should be golden. But, we hope for the best and plan for the worst so let's be super conservative with our projections.

Let's assume a 50% closing rate of a qualified prospect, already educated by your Champion on the value of your solution to their problem. 50% of 40 is <u>20</u>. Our goal.

Delivered monthly value to your Champions.

In Chapter 8, we will walk through the monthly practice of managing Champions. Suffice to say, you want to feed and water them appropriately. The goal is to learn how to keep these relationships mutually beneficial and when you do misstep (and trust me you will), you can correct it immediately, preserve the connection, and not repeat the mistake.

- You must become the BEST CHAMPION of your group of Champions.

- You must always lead by example.

- You must become valuable and indispensable to them.

- You must model the behaviours for them.

When I first started using this strategy myself, I had a Champion who made a very strategic and valuable introduction for me. From that introduction, I got a few more connections (digging deeper into an organisation) and ended up surfacing with a substantial contract.

So excited about closing it, I went right into planning, resource allocation, and my other systems for managing the project. What I failed to do was tell my Champion about the outcome of their introduction.

Months later, they heard from the contact they had introduced me to, about the contract and that we were working together. The Champion called me and gave me hell for not having the courtesy to let him know and to thank them. With no defense to my crappy behaviour, I admitted my misstep and asked for forgiveness. He forgave me, but that Champion was never the same. I blew it because my excitement over the opportunity blinded me from taking a moment to show appreciation for what he did for me in the first place.

I learned a precious and expensive lesson on the proper handling of Champions who take time out of their lives to move you further in your business. This mistake is one I have not repeated since, nor will I in the future.

How many hundreds of thousands of dollars did that mistake cost me in future opportunities? Plus, it was a dick move on my part. As you note my insistence on sticking to the exact recipe of this strategy, you may understand the importance I put upon it being executed as flawlessly as possible. Every day I see people that I Champion who blow it with me. I don't go out of my way to correct their behaviour. Instead, I just stop championing them.

In the last year, I had a broker in my network, whom I introduced to another professional who is a super-connector. The broker did a deal with my contact, yet didn't have the courtesy to thank me for making the introduction in the first place, even though she made thousands of dollars through the transactions. Both myself and the person I introduced them to, are no longer bringing up their name when opportunities arise, and instead suggesting someone else. A costly mistake. Especially given that the person who did business with them, after my introduction, refers out 20–40 transactions a year.

Let's call it $150,000–$200,000 a year in fees that are gone — an expensive and unnecessary mistake.

Easily avoided with a little bit of attention and appreciation. Don't repeat this mistake.

Chapter 4:

The Selection Process of Choosing Your Champions

As you may have already concluded, choosing the right Champions for your business model is essential. It offers both a measurable return on your time and your money.

It also makes it easy for you to Champion them effectively and measurably in return. Setting the first milestone in this strategy of finding and activating 10 Champions, prepare yourself to kiss many frogs to find the princes and princesses. As you prospect Champions in a focused way, you will begin to see characteristics that make some attractive, while allowing you to pass on others. The 'secret sauce' that makes a Champion impactful for your business model will start to present itself over the first 90 days or so.

That said, some characteristics make ALL Champions attractive, regardless of the business model. These are the features that we are most interested in as we build our stable.

Is it possible to have a world-class Champion that is missing one or more of these characteristics? Yes. But we are looking for the complete package whenever possible. These 'unicorns' will have the most significant impact on your business model and your bottom line.

Here is my version of the Super 8 characteristics we are looking for in our Champions. I'm ranking them from most important to least important, but please consider them ALL critical. The most important ones we cannot overlook; the lesser important ones we can live without if they are fantastic everywhere else. Here they are:

1) They influence your niche market(s).

2) They have an established network of contacts.

3) They have a solid reputation

4) They are extroverted.

5) They are articulate and can learn the Three Questions.

6) They are active in their markets.

7) You have an established relationship with them.

8) You can champion them effectively.

You are going to use these eight characteristics to measure the ability of your prospective Champions to serve your business model. You'll notice that your ability to champion them is the eighth factor. While important, you consider this after determining what they can do for you. No point investing time into figuring out how to work for them IF you don't think they are a viable Champion prospect for you. You are selfishly selfless in this phase. It is essential to support our Champions, but that comes last in this assessment phase and first in our execution phase.

For each of these Champion characteristics, I will explain what we are assessing and how to rank each prospective Champion out of a possible score of 10.

1/10 is dog poop; 10/10 is the second coming and could be no better — a real unicorn.

You want Champions to score at least 60 points or higher when combining the eight categories. Assessing this way allows you a bit more objectivity, although not a perfect science by any means.

Remember that Champions can get stronger for you as they get more active on your behalf and you on theirs. There is a growing phase for this relationship.

- You will create opportunities for each other.

- You will both manage these opportunities.

- You will invite and give feedback to each other.

- You will adjust your engagement over time.

As the relationship and learning phase evolves, the level and quality of opportunity will become more significant because you will both know who you should be talking to and whom to act as a gatekeeper on each others' behalf.

Here's a breakdown of the characteristics we are looking to assess so you know how to consider and score for each.

1. They influence your niche market(s).

Your Champions must be able to influence your niche market(s) on your behalf. Whether it be getting access to relevant information or encouraging a qualified prospect to sit/chat with you, they need to have the 'Jedi mind power' over the organizations, groups, and individuals that are within your niche markets.

Some Champions focus in on one particular market; others may influence all your markets. Others still may have access to markets you haven't considered yet but may do so in the future.

I like to track what markets my Champions have this influence over. If I need to swap out a niche market, I look at what markets my Champions are already in that I might want to enter.

How to grade a prospective Champion in this area.

Questions to consider during your assessment:

- Who sees this person as an expert?

- What is it about them that positions them as a thought leader?

- How long have they influenced this/these market(s)?

- Who else holds their stature in these markets? Who has higher stature? Who is an up-and-comer?

- How do they exert their influence over the market(s)?

- How often are they sought out as a market resource?

- How far/deep is their reach and in what areas?

Example of a 10/10 in this area:

The industry as a whole recognizes this person as an expert and trusted source of information. They have years of experience and are often called upon by that market to give an opinion, advice, and to forecast what is to come. They have been a leader in this market for over ten years. They are probably the top five thought leaders in this space and may already be at the top.

They share information online, through commentary at industry events, offering training and keynotes at industry conferences, and are quoted by other respected professionals in this space. When this market wants to know what is happening or what to do, this person is the preferred commentator.

Someone resembling most of these qualities would be awesome, so keep on the lookout for this person. They exist and are rarely activated as Champions because people think they are too busy, hard to get a hold of, or wouldn't be interested — all untrue for the most part.

2. They have an established network of contacts (and growing).

It's not enough that your Champion influences the market, but you also want them to have actual humans they have relationships with. These connections, in your niches, can give you work, create opportunities, and become Champions themselves.

Champions need to have actual relationships where they can call or email on your behalf and connect you with the key people.

Let's use the Healthcare space as a way to illustrate an example. You may be targeting clinics with <20 doctors in their group. Your Champion is a well-regarded and respected physician that teaches doctors a particular procedure.

They have established relationships with actual doctors, practice managers, and complimentary service providers in this target market. They are in a position to make one-to-one introductions on your behalf.

These introductions hold weight because the source of the introduction has credibility and respect from both parties. It is seamless and straight forward.

How to grade a prospective Champion in this area.

Questions to consider during your assessment:

- How many people are they connected with on LinkedIn and other social media platforms? (we want to know if they 'collect' people).

- When attending industry events, how popular are they? Do people seek them out to chat?

- Do key people in each market know them and have an existing relationship with them?

- Do they seem to have inside access to the key players in the market?

- Are they spending time with the key people one on one?

- Do they seem to be collecting new people and actively being introduced to more and more people?

- When at events, do you notice people bringing up others to introduce them? Or do you see them working like a matchmaker putting people together for conversations?

Example of a 10/10 in this area:

A unicorn in this area acts as the host of a party when engaging the market. They make sure people are feeling respected, influential, and engaged. They tell people that there 'is someone they have to meet,' and then facilitate the introduction to make it happen. They take people over to others and make the introductions in real-time. There is always someone coming up to them and saying, "sorry to interrupt...but I wanted to say hi. Let's connect soon."

You'll notice that others want the Champion to know that they see them (and to be seen by them), want to spend time with them, and are looking forward to connecting with them. They are a valuable commodity and always have a full 'dance card.'

3. They have a solid reputation.

It's possible to have a Champion who has massive influence over your niche market(s) and has a tonne of personal connections, but who isn't respected by people you are looking to convert.

Birds of a feather flock together.

If your Champion is an arse, you will likely get painted by that same brush. This 'first impression' can prove to be challenging to overcome. Look carefully at how that Champion is perceived by your niche and determine if they are the person you want co-signing your reputation.

If everyone loves them, the market will want to love you too. If everyone fears or detests your Champion, the market may meet with you to avoid blowback, but not want to do business with you. This situation is terrible. You want people to meet with you because they see a selfish benefit, not because of some servitude they are paying towards your Champion.

In short, you want Champions who are benevolent, servant leaders. Professionals who look to leave people better than they find them. If you find that, you are way ahead in the game. A solid reputation comes from serving people in a measurable and meaningful way. Surround yourself with those people, and you get the benefit of their work and can model that behaviour yourself. Make your Champion stable an A**hole−free zone.

How to grade a prospective Champion in this area.

Questions to consider during your assessment:

- What did you hear about the Champion before you met them?

- How do you describe them to others?

- What types of people are in their inner circle? Good people or challenging personalities?

- How do they serve others?

- Do they look for win/win in all situations?

- How do they deal with conflict? Emotional or practical?

- How are they critical about others?

- Do they gossip or say unkind things?

- How do they warn people about things?

- How do they give feedback to others?

- What negative things have you heard about this person? Are they founded in any truth?

- Who are their critics?

- What criticisms would others have about them?

Example of a 10/10 in this area:

A top Champion in this area would be a builder of people. They aren't afraid to get their hands dirty and help out. People who have never met them have good things to say about them because of what others have told them. When someone is unkind, this Champion either stands up for the target, changes the subject, or respectfully addresses the situation in another way. They don't make others wrong to be right. They are the mediator between challenging situations. Even the crankiest person in the room likes and respects them. They are kind when others wouldn't be.

4. They are extroverted.

I'm sorry, Introverts. If you are part of that clan, take a breath, and I'll get to the benefits of Introverted Champions before we are done.

My preference is choosing Extroverts as Champions. They like to talk to lots of people and get their juice from human interaction. These are the evangelists of business models. They are Circus Barkers. I love it when my Champions use me, my business model, or my books as a discussion point with other people. They do this automatically and with ease. They are up to talking to anyone and everyone about anything. They like being the centre of attention. They love telling people what movies are good, restaurants they should visit, the best airlines to fly on, the hottest vacation spots to explore, and new cars to test drive. They like sharing their opinion and know-how to steer a conversation to a topic they want to share.

Extroverts also tend to want to solve other peoples' challenges and offer up solutions. If they have a solid reputation and influence, these solutions hold substantial weight. This natural tendency is good for business prospecting. The only challenge is to ensure you give them the right script of things to share. Going off-script can be problematic. For all the opportunities that Extrovert Champions have produced for me, there is always some re-educating of the prospect if the extroverted Champion went out on a tangent.

Now for the Introverts. Not to be discounted, they can also play an essential role as Champions but more in different ways. My Introverted Champions produce about 50% of the qualified client prospects but almost double the other Champion prospects. Most of my Extroverted Champions came through

Introverted Champions. Without my Introverts, I wouldn't have met most of my Extroverts. I think they do this so they don't have to talk to either of us.

As well, my Introverts are excellent at market observations and assessing dynamics, but only when I ask for it. And I have to be mindful to ask.

How to grade a prospective Champion in this area.

Questions to consider during your assessment:

- How does this person 'show up' in public settings? Engaged or like a cat getting a bath?

- Do they seem energized or drained by talking with lots of people.

- Do they offer their opinion on things or are they more reserved and wait to be asked?

- Do they seek out chances to connect with people/peers, or are they less likely to do this?

- At a networking event or industry activity, how do they work the room? Walk around or stand in one spot?

- Are they quick to talk to strangers or more reserved?

- Are they sought out for their opinion by others? Does everyone get excited when they show up to things (like the party has started)?

Example of a 10/10 in this area:

My friend, Damon Pallan, is a 10/10 in this area. Whether you go out for lunch with him, go golfing, or walking down the street, he is like the mayor. He knows everyone, people go out of their way to come and talk to him, and you can see their faces brighten when they see him walk into a room. He gets energized by talking to people and is honestly interested in how everyone is doing. Anytime I need a recommendation, he has many and is happy to make introductions to these solutions as soon as I ask him, no matter how busy he is. He sets a high bar for all professionals.

5. They are articulate and can learn the Three Questions.

There's nothing worse than a Champion, whom you have educated and activated, who mumbles through the answers to your Three Questions. It's soul-crushing to watch because you witness the viable opportunity vaporize right in front of your eyes because they miss the messaging.

Even worse is meeting with someone that your Champion introduced, and they go on to tell you what they think you do only for you to have to correct them on what your actual business model is.

If your Champion is usually very articulate and clear in with how they communicate things, you likely haven't activated them properly with your information (shame!). If they sometimes talk like they have marbles in their mouth, off the cuff, or don't always make much sense, time to swap them out for someone else.

It's better not to have them as a Champion, than to have them do it poorly. If you don't get qualified prospects through your Champions, they have not trained properly, or the Champion can't articulate information succinctly. It doesn't make them a terrible person; it just makes them a lousy Champion. Put a bullet in the relationship and move on. It's more trouble than it's worth.

How to grade a prospective Champion in this area.

Questions to consider during your assessment:

- How do they describe other products or services? Does their description make you more or less likely to find out more?

- When they are telling a story, is it easy to follow and relevant?

- Do they use clear and accessible language or do they have 'smart–guy–itis' using industry jargon?

- When they describe products or services that you know, does their description seem accurate?

- When you have had them introduce you to others, did the description match who the person is and what they do? If not, how far off were they? Remember that not all Champions who struggle with this are bad; they may not have the right activation. The onus is on the person being championed, not the Champion, to ensure this has been done correctly.

Example of a 10/10 in this area:

When you are assessing a Champion in this, a top one will be on-brand with everything they describe. You'll note in how they convey messaging if you are more or less likely to check something out, given their description of it. If they set your expectations and then meet your expectations in how they describe things, you are probably golden. This characteristic can be a bit harder to judge before you activate them, but keep a close eye to appreciate what you are working with fully.

6. They are active in the markets.

You want your Champions to be active in your markets. If they have been out of the market for a while, their credibility starts to lose its power. The best Champions are in the game. They are considered to be 'a player,' not a 'used to be' player.

To illustrate, let's consider a Champion in the legal field. You probably want someone at the top of their game, who is writing new case law, and leading the industry in how the law is practiced. Not someone who was a big deal in the '80s and now attending events and lunches to 'visit with people'. Not to say there isn't some value in that person, but there is a 'best by' date on Champions. Still good to leverage older ones, but fresh and dynamic ones are preferred, plus it's more comfortable for you to champion them if they are active. It is much harder to champion others who don't have a lot going on.

How to grade a prospective Champion in this area.

Questions to consider during your assessment:

- How current are they in your market(s)?

- Does the market still see them as relevant and representing what is going on today?

- Are they on the upswing or cresting and heading downhill in regards to relevance?

- How much more runway do they have before someone displaces them?

- How much do others model their activities on this person?

- Do others use them as a benchmark?

Example of a 10/10 in this area:

One of my Champions is a young(ish) partner at a major West Coast Consulting firm. She's developing new procurement and supply chain management systems all the time for her clients while being a killer in business development. Many months she writes more business than the rest of her local partners combined, and on top of that, hosts monthly seminars (internal) for colleagues and (external) for her clients and her Champions. She is in a constant state of innovation and is carefully watched by partners, underlings, clients, alliances, and the industry as a whole. When she has an idea or wants to share a best practice, the markets listen carefully and follow her lead. One of her more established partners said to me, "she is the future of this firm and this industry". Pretty strong and well-earned accolades from someone who used to be the innovator of the industry and now happy to support her as she takes it to the next level.

7. You have an established relationship with them.

With all Champions, the more they like and trust you, the more likely they are to refer you to the right prospects and contacts. As your relationship evolves, Champions become better for you and your business model. That said, some new Champions can also come out of the gates super fast. They see what you offer adds value to their contacts and makes them look good, so they shotgun you out into the market.

On the other end of the spectrum, some of your long-term business relationships may not produce any opportunities even though like and trust is in place. This difference in outcome is just the nature of the beast.

Sometimes people have seen us one way for so long (and we haven't corrected it) that it is impossible to re-program them to who you are today. New contacts are easier to educate because they don't come with preconceptions. They may need time to understand you and your business model to become active. As long as you see movement in the right direction, continue to invest time and attention in this.

Regardless if someone comes on fast, or takes their time to get active, don't take it personally. If someone you've known forever doesn't produce, it might not be their forte.

If someone new understands and can articulate but wants to wait a while before opening up their network, that's okay too. Their reputation is their currency, and they may wish to observe you before endorsing you. Their reputation took years to create. Having you blow it for them isn't optimal, so they may need time. Give it to them.

Because every Champion will onboard differently, we are always identifying and inventorying Champions, just like prospects. Some will move fast; some will move slow. We stay in a constant state of recruiting.

Our business is not dependent on any one Champion or client. Your most active Champion this year may be your weakest next year, so always look for the future, best Champion to add to your team.

How to grade a prospective Champion in this area.

Questions to consider during your assessment:

- How long have I known them?

- Is trust established? If so, how was it built? If not, what needs to happen to establish trust?

- Do they have feedback from clients/qualified sources to speak to the quality of your service/product?

- What information do they need professionally to understand your solution?

- Have we championed them yet? If so, what did we do, and how did it end up?

- Are we modelling the Champion behaviour for them?

- Can we ask them what they need to be the best version of a Champion for us?

- Do they see us in the right light and the correct position?

Example of a 10/10 in this area:

A few years back, I met a lawyer in Seattle who worked in the tech space. Her firm was well known for incorporating some major global tech companies we all know. We had been connected through another Champion, and had a pleasant visit at the Seattle Fairmont Hotel.

I immediately assessed her as being Introverted and rather than looking to activate her to source prospective clients for us, I wanted to position her to give me industry feedback. In turn, I could Champion her by introducing her to technology clients we were currently working with. Years after knowing each other and running in the same circles, she said to me over coffee, "Do you ever work with Senior Associates to bring in business?"

I told her, "Yes, we do this all the time."

She said, "How often do you make your way down into Oregon and California?"

I told her, "Regularly and I'm touring from Bellingham, Washington to San Diego, California later this spring."

She told me she wanted to introduce me to some of her partners and associates so that I could meet with them during my upcoming tour. Please remember that this was a new Champion, we just started 'dating' and she was super Introverted. Over the next two weeks, she introduced me to 41 partners and associates in 13 offices. Many of these professionals became clients or Champions and introduced us to more clients and Champions. She came out of the gate hot and now we send back and forth 2–3 opportunities per month each. Never underestimate a hot start. It doesn't always happen, but sometimes it does. Be open to the chance and be patient should it take some time. All are valuable. Focus on the outcome rather than a specific timeline.

8. You can Champion them effectively.

Golden Rule: To have good Champions, you need to be a good Champion. All Champions you recruit also need to have you champion them. You have to discover what they need that you can offer. In most cases, it could be looking for opportunities for each other and making connections. Maybe you give them industry insight or act as a sounding board. It all depends on what they need. I have some Champions that aren't in a sales role. So they may ask me to review their training/marketing plan, read through something and give feedback, or give my opinion on a business idea they have. All are easy to do, and I'm happy to accommodate for all they do for me. Sometimes they need to know something that I don't know. But I know someone that has the answers, and I quickly make the introduction.

It cannot be one-sided...ever. I can count on one hand how many people have said to me in the last year, 'what can I do for you?' Instead, they tell me what they are going to do for me and my clients/contacts, which happens to be me/us buying something that they are selling. It just doesn't play. Everyone takes that approach, and it's all 'leg humpy.'

How to grade a prospective Champion in this area.

Questions to consider during your assessment:

- Do I understand what I can do for them that will have a measurable benefit to them?

- Do I understand what they do that is different from their peers?

- Have they clearly articulated to me what they are looking for so I know how to keep an eye out for it?

- Do I have people in my current network that would benefit from knowing this Champion?

- Am I clear on what they struggle with that I might be able to alleviate?

- Do I want to be associated with this person? Put my reputation on the line for them, and put the time into Championing them on an ongoing basis?

- Can I get them to clearly articulate the answers to the Three Questions to make my work simpler to accomplish?

- Do I want to share this book with them?

Example of a 10/10 in this area:

My friend and colleague Harp Sandhu is a Wealth Manager at Raymond James. I've gotten to know him well over the past few years. A Champion introduced us. Harp is meticulous in his management of clients, but one area in particular where he stands out is working with clients who have a cross border issue. It could be a Canadian repatriating to Canada after working in the US. Could be a Canadian child inheriting money from a US parent. Rather than liquidating the money in the US, paying a big chunk to the IRS and getting the remainder, Harp has the ability, through his platform, to avoid a big part of this tax issue.

When I'm in the US working with accountants and lawyers, I let them know about him and this solution and offer to make the introduction. As well, any clients who are Canadian that are also working in the US, I let them know that if/when they come home, to reach out to Harp to help them get their assets back into the country. He's helped our clients bring back their cars, home stuff, and even whisky collections. I have people like this strategically positioned throughout Canada that I can Champion (quickly) and who Champion me. It's easy because I know/like/trust them, I am out engaging in these markets anyways, I always meet fellow Canadians in my business circles, and I know Harp will make me look good to these people by offering a solution they didn't previously know existed.

Note: Great Champions are great salespeople (of course, they will be selling you), and there is nothing salespeople hate more than someone selling something poorly. I want a selfish benefit if I'm going to be your Champion and expect you to want the same. I'm going to give you what you want, and you are going to give me what I want, and we are going to keep doing that because we like what we are each getting. Win/win. Nobody is doing each other a favour. It's a mutually beneficial, selfish relationship.

That's why it's sustainable and scalable. When this is your focus, your Champions stay long term.

Be mindful that because they may not have read this book or had access to it, you are going to need to work with them to extrapolate what it is that they do, why it matters, and who cares so you can put them in front of clients, contacts, and opportunities as they come across you. Hell, give them this copy of the book and have them read it.

Let me tell you what's going through your head. "I don't know that I have clients for them!" "What if I can't offer them value?" Hold your horses. In the next section, we are going to cover all the usual objections/fears professionals have in implementing the Champion Strategy. The fear, concern, or hesitation you have is all based on a false story you have been or will be telling yourself. We'll sort that stuff out next, so you don't sabotage this brilliant business development strategy. Let's just jump into it now. Turn the page.

Chapter 5:

Overcoming Objections: Yours and Theirs

After the excitement of 'what Champions can deliver, 'people tend to freak out around having the initial conversations with people.

"What if I get it wrong?"

"What if they say no?"

"What if they are already Championing someone else?

"What if they say yes and I don't have any clients for them."

They start to play dialogue in their heads of all the ways this strategy could go wrong. Maybe I can't produce for them. Perhaps they can't deliver for me. What if I make them feel uncomfortable for asking?

All of these ideas are based in fear. And this fear of what might happen (which is super unlikely to happen). We tend to get inside our own heads with new things and start to create false narratives on what will happen, without any basis in the real world or experience doing this particular thing. They may be connecting with other times in the past, where they thought they were in the position to be Championed, and the other person didn't come through. They were disappointed. They were mad. They were hurt.

Fear of rejection is a powerful force. I've always found it crazy that someone would avoid asking someone for help, rather than to ask them and have them say 'no. 'The worst–case scenario in this is that the person doesn't help you, which is the exact position you are in now. It can't get worse, only better. Let's agree that up until now, you probably haven't been super articulate with what you do, why it matters, and who cares. You may have been targeting everyone instead of three select markets. Honestly, you have been hard to Champion. Let's remember the three reasons people don't refer you:

1) They don't know you are looking.

2) They don't know what to say because you haven't fed them your information.

3) They think you are an a**hole.

By implementing the strategy and talking with them, you remedy #'s 1 & 2. If the reason is #3...well, then nothing we are going to do will change that in the short term.

What I have found in my practice, working with clients since 1999, is they have two sets of 'objections 'they need to overcome. Internal objections they struggle with and perceived objections they think prospective Champions will have.

The first set of objections (the ones in your head) will feel very real, but are false in almost ALL cases. We are going to address these first so you can see how your mind will sabotage your efforts if you let them. The second set of objections (the ones you think prospective Champions will have) are also false. We will go through how to address each one of them, even though I'm 99% certain you will not hear one of these objections in your activation of Champions. If you do come across one, you will be prepared to address them. Forewarned is forearmed, but I'm telling you, it is very, very, very unlikely that you will hear any objections. The list I will present to you are all derived from what clients thought people would say, but that they never actually heard.

The internal objections you will face when putting this strategy into place, include:

What if I activate a Champion I can't be a Champion for?

What if they don't have the quality leads I'm looking for?

What if they do something that I don't want to be associated with?

What if they fail to produce anything for me?

What if they already have someone they are sending referrals to/being a Champion for?

What if they aren't in business building mode?

What if they aren't the best communicator?

I've known them for a long time, and they haven't sent me anyone.

I don't think they even know what I do.

I don't think they can understand what I do.

We will address each of these objections one by one, so you can get your head calibrated to make this as successful as it needs to be.

The objections prospective Champions might say to you as you broach the subject with them include:

I'm not that active in the business.

I don't know who I'd send to you.

I don't want other people to think I'm showing favouritism.

I already have established relationships with people who do what you do.

I don't know if giving your information is fair to others.

I'm trying to dial things down. I don't want more responsibility.

I'm not allowed to make recommendations (lawyer/government).

I don't know if I'm comfortable doing that yet.

I think you should do it on your own.

I wouldn't know where to start.

I don't want to disappoint you.

All of these objections are important to us to feel prepared for anything. Knowing what could be said (but likely won't) allows us to tailor our messaging (internal to ourselves and external to others) to bypass any roadblocks that will present themselves. We MUST overcome our internal objections first as they WILL prevent us from launching this strategy.

Overcoming objections with others isn't as straightforward. Should we get an objection, we don't want to convince anyone of why they should be our Champion. It looks desperate. Instead, we want to educate them on the selfish benefit they get from being our Champion, and after addressing any objections they may (or may not) verbalize, we look to see what the outcome is.

For some, they will jump on the bandwagon right away. Others will need to ask additional questions to assure themselves they will do a good job. Others may dip a toe in the pool but not fully commit. And the final group will be split into two: half who will say they will do it and won't, and the other half who will tell you they simply won't be able to do it.

This last group is critical to us because we don't want to put resources towards a group that has no intention to play the Champion role for us. They give us a gift by being honest about not wanting to do it. If they act as if they will, but don't, it will take additional resources from us to figure this out on our own.

The thing to remember with this last group is sometimes they come around. They see you being championed by others (and you championing them), and they want to get in on the action. There is a strong social pull to being included, and when they see you have profitable, mutually beneficial relationships (especially with their competitors), they may have a change of heart. These people tend to become the best Champions. They now have to 'earn 'what was once offered to them for free. Don't dismiss them entirely, but do limit the support/time you invest in them until they become an active player in your circle.

Remember that 'no 'almost always means 'I don't understand 'or 'not right now'.

I've spent much time on this chapter (as you will be able to tell by the length of it) to address each objection (internal and external) and how to think it through. Once you understand the objections you are most likely to come across, you can practice the proper answer, which addresses the objection professionally. We aren't looking to convince anyone of anything, including yourself. You have value. You are looking for people who add value to you and you to them. Simple.

Internal Objections

"What if I activate a Champion I can't be a Champion for?"

You won't do this. Remember the test that we conduct before we engage a Champion. If you feel you are unable to champion them, then don't pursue them as a Champion in the first place. They can still be in your sphere of influence, just not in this particular role.

But ask yourself why. Why are you unable to be their Champion? Are they untrustworthy? Do they have a bad reputation? Are they bad at what they do? Do they rub people wrong? Are you unsure of what they do? Are you unsure HOW to champion them? Do you have someone already in the mix that is a direct competitor for them, and you don't want to be seen as being in both camps?

Spend some time thinking through your rationale and see if there is a way you can work through it or what would need to be in place (or omitted) for you to feel comfortable championing them.

"What if they don't have the quality leads I'm looking for?"

It's possible but unlikely. Everyone you meet in business IS a client or KNOWS a client. An activated Champion, if not hiding in a hole 23 hours a day, will come across prospects that will be a fit for you. My guess is they are already coming across qualified opportunities for you weekly, but because you haven't activated (educated) them, those leads are just walking past.

Assume that they have the qualified leads you are looking for, and you'll find it becomes a reality. If the Champion is active in promoting you AND they are engaged in your niche market(s), they would have to work hard to NOT find leads for you. Will it happen every day or week? No. But will it happen monthly? Most definitely. That's why we have multiple Champions activated in place, just like having various fishing rods in the water with various lures. You increase your chances of filling the boat with more options in the water. But you don't catch anything if you don't put those lines in the water. Ask, and you shall receive.

"What if they do something that I don't want to be associated with?"

This situation has happened to me many times. It's generally around a great Champion who is in the multi-level marketing space. It gets a bad rap (i.e. Amway), but truthfully, MLM is an excellent way for a would-be entrepreneur to get some business training and experience with a proven model.

That said, there can be some 'leg humping' associated with these models, totally dependent on the person who is recruiting a downline (people downstream from them in the business).

I'm honest with my Champions in this space. I'm not going to introduce them to top clients or prospects because it is going to be off-brand for what we do. But I will connect them to young entrepreneurs or professionals looking to dip a toe in the world of being an entrepreneur and not sure what they want to do. These aren't our markets, but these two groups ask us many questions, and I do believe that MLM offers a valuable opportunity to make money and learn how to sell, recruit, and present on a model that someone else has done all the guesswork around.

I'm clear, as the Champion, what I will and will not do in my role. Then it is up to the person I'm championing to determine if they'd like to take me at what I'm offering or not. They always do, and there are no hard feelings that I'm not opening up my A-level clients/contacts to them.

Honesty and transparency is key to a Champion relationship. Be prepared to have (and hear) the hard conversations, so there are no misunderstandings.

"*What if they fail to produce anything for me?*"

Well, that would be the worst–case scenario, wouldn't it? And assuming they aren't producing anything for you now, there is only an upside to having this conversation. As I've shared before, there are only three reasons they won't pass on opportunities for you.

They probably don't know what you are looking for or that you are looking at all. This ceases to be an issue when you tell them about the niche market(s) you serve and answer the three questions for them. Problem solved.

They don't know what to say. Again, you will tell them what to say. Problem solved.

They think you are an a**hole. Sorry, I can't help with that. You'll have to sort that out on your own.

"What if they already have someone they are sending referrals to or being a Champion for?"

This is excellent news! It means they know how to do what we are asking them to do. Now we just have to redirect some of their attention to us from their current target. How? Simple. We have the Champion conversation, and we focus on the following points:

- What a Champion is.

- Your intention to have them be your Champion.

- Your intention to become their Champion.

- You acknowledging they have a current relationship but would like to be the back up to that person.

- You will go first by championing them.

The reason we approach it this way is excellent Champions rarely get reciprocation from those they support. They may get a 'thanks 'or a 'lunch 'every once in a while. When a new player shows up on the scene and is a Champion to that person, it is hard not to start to focus more on the person feeding them opportunities than the one who just says 'thanks 'or drops off a bottle of wine.

Here's how we put this into play. First, we share with them the niche market(s) we are going after (as we do with all Champions), and we answer the Three Questions (likely not what the person they are currently championing provided). Doing just these two things puts us in a league of our own. Then we find out from them what markets they are going after, how they answer the Three Questions, and what they need.

After we know they know what our model is, and we are clear on what their needs are, we model the behaviour. We deliver something of 'value 'to them first, to give them a 'taste 'of what could be. As soon as you do this, you put an enormous amount of pressure on the existing relationship. You'll find your prospective Champion becomes much more 'critical ' of the lack of balance in their current relationship.

Should you do something for your prospective Champion, and it isn't reciprocated, let it go. You've given them a taste of what things look like for people that work with you. Let them stay in the existing relationship, and when there is an opening, they may circle back. We don't continue to feed them if it doesn't look like anything is coming back. Everyone gets a taste, once.

I had a mortgage broker client who entered a new market that was packed with competition. She went out to meet with realtors to find some Champions. Many of them had relationships with mortgage brokers that dated back to elementary school (Oy!). So we changed tack.

What she said to the realtors is:

"I know you have your regular person from 9 AM– 5 PM. Let me be your person from 5 PM–9 AM. I can pre-approve people that might come for a night showing.

I'm happy to work on your open houses with you. I can be an extra set of hands and prequalify people on the spot.

I'm open on all holidays and weekends. So when your #1 isn't available, and you are worried that a deal might fall without financing in place, use me.

As well, if your #1 choice for mortgages is on holidays, unavailable, or super busy, use me as the overflow."

One would think that these realtors would have gone back to their existing mortgage brokers, shared what was talked about with my client, and these current mortgage brokers would offer to do the same. Do you know how many adjusted their approach?

Not one. Zilch. Zero. Nada.

So, as part of our strategy, she stopped working 9 AM–5 PM and started working 5 PM to 9 AM and all weekends and holidays. She wrote, on average, 20–30 mortgages a month. All her business, aside from her business development, came from Champions who already had mortgage broker relationships.

We've duplicated this Champion strategy with hundreds of other brokers in secondary markets over the last twenty years, to great success. And every time, these mortgage brokers ended up becoming the Realtors #1 contact.

*Note: Where this strategy doesn't work as well (or at all) is in the case of family relationships. Spouses, siblings, cousins are hard to displace due to social consequences, so our recommendation is to leave those relationships where they are. You can still talk with that person once, but unless there is a family meltdown, you are unlikely to get traction. As well, in this case, don't do the initial Champion activity to give them a taste. The ROI on this effort will be very low and best to keep your 'leverage 'for qualified prospective Champions.

Simply acknowledge that you appreciate the family dynamic and should that person stop operating in your business space, you'd welcome the opportunity to work together. Then leave it alone.

"What if they aren't in business building mode?"

Not a deal-breaker. We want people that are active in the markets, and some of the best Champions may already have a full business model. A great situation to be in. As long as they are still attending events, talking to people, well respected, and relevant, they are still valuable to you. What you want to consider is how you can Champion them. What do they need support with to make their life (work or personal) easier? This can be a great conversation topic.

Some Champions just want to give back, but in my experience, this isn't enough. You will need to sort out what you can do for them so that their championing of you become an ongoing activity. Ask lots of great questions of these people and look to see where you can lessen or alleviate any pressure they may be facing or who can you introduce them to that can do so.

One of my Champions was in this situation. Full business model, great staff, tonnes of money, but the thing I found out she struggled with was childcare. At the time, I had a stake in a nanny service and also in a babysitter match-making service. Once I found out her struggles with having the kids watched, we got her sorted right away. It was the one thing she consistently struggled with and worried about. And something I solved with two phone calls. That bought me sufficient currency with her for years to come. That said, I still searched every month at how to add value to our relationship to keep her engaged. It's an ongoing practice, not a 'set it and forget it 'type situation.

"What if they aren't the best communicator?"

This is a bit more important, but it all depends on what you need. You don't need someone who is a public speaker. You want someone articulate and who can convey messaging with ease. I usually look at how someone describes other businesses, vacations, or experiences. Are they engaging or are they dull? Even dull can produce results, but we are looking for original and engaging storytellers who captivate an audience. These 'types 'provide the most significant results for us.

"I've known them for a long time, and they haven't sent me anyone."

Not surprising. Assuming they don't think you're an arse, then they either don't know you are looking, or they don't know what to say. Let's remove those barriers from the equation and see what happens. And don't forget the power of having the actual Champion conversation with them and setting the intention for it being ongoing and mutually beneficial.

*Have you been an excellent Champion to them over the time you've known each other? Can you clearly articulate what they do or what they need? Remember, we must model the behaviour so that they can measure against us.

"I don't think they even know what I do."

Great! Clean slate and something we can remedy, now that we have completed our pre-work. Sit down with them and let them know the niche markets we serve, the solutions we provide, and how we answer the Three Questions. Training is way easier than re-training. This is a gift. Take advantage of it. They will appreciate you taking the time.

"I don't think they can understand what I do."

As Einstein said, "If you can't explain it simply, you likely don't understand it well enough." As someone who has spent the last two decades watching tens of thousands of clients stumble through the Three Questions, I want you to take responsibility first before passing judgement on your prospective Champion. Our Three Questions needs to be understood by a ten-year-old. If they can't be, we haven't done enough work with them yet.

Once you have completed your Three Questions for your niche market(s), have the conversation with them. Test them, after you describe what you do, to determine their level of understanding. I think you will be pleasantly surprised when they seem relieved to understand what it is you do finally. You'll know you hit the jackpot when there is a flicker in their eyes when everything 'clicks.'

"What happens if that flicker doesn't come?"

You might have a dud of a prospective Champion, but I'd estimate the chance of that to be less than 1/100 of the people you talk to.

If they tick all the other boxes we are looking for in our Champions (the Selection process we covered in Chapter 4), it is unlikely you have a dud. But if you are confident that your Three Questions are on point and this particular Champion isn't firing after a clear explanation on your part...move on.

As I hope you can see, the stories you are telling yourself (or will tell yourself) are not grounded in any truth. To look at things objectively, we are merely searching out like–minded people whom we can work with to promote each others 'interests. People have been doing this since the dawn of time, only this is intentional rather than hoping it will naturally happen. We are creating an environment for which to develop a successful relationship for all involved. We aren't asking for anything; we are offering. We are modelling the behaviour.

Remember that most professionals feel isolated, even those on teams. In this strategy, we are developing relationships that will be held in high regard and reverence by all that engage.

Now let's look at the things we 'think 'people might say. It will be rare to get any of these objections. If you do, you'll know how to handle them. Fear should disappear when you are prepared and remember, anyone that doesn't want to be your Champion is missing out. As you further this strategy and your networks continue to evolve, you go from looking for unicorns to becoming the unicorn.

External Objections

"I'm not that active in the business."

Having influence over markets and established relationships is more important than being super active in markets. Champions who are seen as having high credibility and integrity are more valuable than junior people who are out hustling and in the process of making a name for themselves. As long as the prospective Champion is still respected and relevant, they could offer you much value.

Remember, Champions are not just those that introduce you or connect you but also act as sounding boards for ideas (leveraging their wisdom) or who know the current 'temperature 'of the market. They know this because they are read up, ear to the grapevine, and are familiar with market dynamics and signals. If a prospective Champion thinks they have to be super active in the business to be a good Champion for you, explain the other roles that Champions can play. Each Champion will specialize in particular functions for you (introducing prospects, introducing other Champions, identifying market dynamics, uncovering opportunities, acting as a sounding board, and others), and this function may shift from time to time. These relationships will naturally evolve, and that's a good thing.

A Champion who makes qualified prospect introductions today may be your most trusted sounding board in five years. This evolution should be welcomed.

Here's how you respond:

"Activity in the market is not as important as influence over the market. The reason I chose you to be my

Champion is the high level of respect I and others have for you. You have wisdom that is valuable to me and the market, and I'm looking to leverage that expertise to guide me as I continue to develop my model. Whether it be meeting prospective clients you come across, being introduced to other professionals you think I should engage, or even giving me your insights on what the market is doing, I welcome any insight, advice, or input you are willing to share with me.

On top of that, I'm committed to being valuable to you not only in being a natural person for you to champion, but modelling the behaviour back to you by supporting any initiatives where you think I can add value."

"I don't know who I'd send to you."

This objection shows up when the Champions don't know who you are targeting or what you are offering. When you face this objection, I want you to hear what they aren't saying, which is: *"You haven't made it clear for me yet who you want me to target for you and what you want me to say."*

Here's how you respond:

"I understand entirely, and the onus is on me to share who I'm looking to meet and why they would want to meet with me. My niche markets are (insert your three niche markets). The market I think you would be particularly powerful for me would be (insert niche market), and the solution that I offer this market is: (insert solution). Does that make sense? So if you hear someone saying things like:

Give them an example (one sentence long).

Give them a second example (one sentence long).

Or

Give them a third example (one sentence long).

You would tell them that you are going to introduce the two of us by email to see if the challenge they are having can be solved by the solutions I offer."

Example:

If I were doing this with a Champion in the Financial Services space, the three examples I might use would look something like this:

"So if you hear someone saying things like:

"I'm having a hard time bringing new assets in."

"My market is shrinking, and I don't know what to do."

"My clients are dying, and their assets are leaving my business and going to their heirs."

You would tell the advisor you are going to connect us. Let them know that I do this all the time. That I can share with them some ideas on how to bring in new money, leverage their existing relationships to source new clients, and how to secure connections with the next generation before their parent/grandparent dies."

I'm trying to give my perspective Champion some business examples of what they may hear in the market that would trigger them to think, "I should connect them with Chris." Then, of course, the Champions would leverage my answers to the three questions that I trained them on.

"Chris specializes in working with Investment Advisors to expand, attract, and retain assets.

This is important because if an Advisor looks like all their competition, all they will do is compete on fees.

Advisors looking to grow a profitable, sustainable, and scalable business are most interested in what he offers."

And we are off to the races.

"I don't want other people to think I'm showing favouritism."

Professionals who get work or opportunities from a variety of sources will be sensitive to not alienate these additional channels by showing favouritism. Imagine you are selling real estate and recommend an Interior Designer to all your clients, only to find out that she gives out the name of one of your competitors when out in the market.

You would be quick to find an alternate source to refer to as you would assume no opportunities would ever be coming back your way. Don't minimise this fear as it is valid and plays out often. You don't want your Champions to have any negative impact from being supportive of you.

Here's how to respond:

"I fully appreciate that and don't want to put you in any type of stressful situation. It might be an option for you to choose three vendors that are targeting this specific niche market and ask them to give you their unique selling proposition. When you come across an opportunity, you can qualify the prospect and point them to the right person.

I've done my homework, and I can clearly outline who I'm the perfect fit for and who I'm not. If the others you support do the same, you'll have a guideline as to which opportunity goes to whom and nobody will gripe because they have given you the type of client they want to work with and the types they don't."

*Having done this strategy for 20+ years, let me tell you how this plays out. You give the Champion your clear description of whom you want to work with, the solution you offer, and why you are the obvious choice for that specific market. He/she may approach the other people in your industry they know (competitors/colleagues) and ask them to identify their ideal client and their unique selling proposition. These people will not do the work. They will either say they will, but won't, or default and say, "just send me anyone looking for 'x."

The script from others would look something like this (using Interior Design as an example),

"I am an Interior Designer.

People need guidance on interior design.

I work with people looking for interior design."

Then you come up and say,

> "*I specialise in working with professionals downsizing and looking to make their new space current and functional.*
>
> *Because professionals are busy, I do all the leg work without them and then bring the   concepts to them for approval. The people I best fit with are busy professionals who will share their design preferences with me, and then I take those concepts and relate them in the real world.*"

Your Champion has a 'get out of jail free' card through your process, and the others have made it much more challenging to place them due to a lack of follow up or clarity. You have made yourself the easy target for professional prospects to be sent to, and the others may get the crumbs. Maybe.

"I already have established relationships with people who do what you do."

The underlying core of this objection is that this prospective Champion is loyal and not quick to displace established relationships. This is a good thing. What proves to be challenging is that to replace their current choice of your profession, you need to respectfully create 'space 'to become the second choice (and then first choice). Do not claim to be better, more skilled, more experienced, or to make a case against the other person/persons (i.e. Do not slam or criticize them). Instead, determine what would need to happen to be the first choice within a particular situation rather than all circumstances. If you can get a foothold in one area, you can expand your influence into others.

Here's how to respond:

"I very much appreciate that you have existing relationships that you trust and feel confident in representing. I don't want to replace or compete with them but instead, possibly add to your tool chest of professionals that you champion. Are there any areas of business that your current professional(s) don't cover that might provide me with an opportunity? If so, what would need to happen for me to earn my way into that particular spot with you to become your person for those opportunities?

Also, are the current relationships reciprocal in the way you would like it to be? Is there a way that I could add value to what you are doing or support things within your business model that would bring me front of mind? I model the Champion behaviours for my Champions and am committed to being as big of a Champion for my circle as they are for me."

If the prospective Champions says that the current person covers everything (unlikely to be true) and that there isn't anything you could do for them that isn't already getting done, thank them. Let them know that you would welcome the opportunity to develop your relationship further if an opportunity comes up. If and when they would like to pick up the conversation, you would certainly appreciate it.

Then what you would do is look for something you could do for that person that would add value without them expecting it. This action will weigh against what their current person/people is/are doing for them and set a benchmark of performance that they would need to meet to remain the first choice.

Here's an example of a practice application I've used to go from 'backup 'to a starter.

A legal Champion prospect had an existing relationship with another sales training organisation that spanned 10+ years. As I was prospecting a Champion, I found out that they referred, on average, ten firms a year to our competitor. They had been happy with the output (as shared by the clients they had referred to this business) and were in no rush to make a switch on whom they referred.

I sat down with the prospective Champion (introduced to me by an existing Champion). After understanding they weren't looking to change, I looked for a segment of the market we might be valuable in...in this case, female lawyers stuck as Senior Associates. I said to the prospective Champion, "At the firm that you refer to, do they have any specialized training for female lawyers at firms stuck at the Senior Associate level?" (This, of course, was a loaded question as I knew our competitors didn't offer this).

She said, "I don't know, but I don't believe so. I think their training is for all lawyers."

I said, "We specialize in working with professional women and have a program to work with female attorneys stuck at Senior Associate level, to make partner within 24 months. Not only do firms not lose their female associates (a substantial financial loss to the firm), but the Associates can often open up opportunities to the firm, not available to male counterparts.

If female lawyers are forced to learn a male model of business development, these opportunities are lost to the firm. Maybe we could be your resource for firms noticing women leaving the firm unexpectedly or uncontrollably and want training that is customized for female opportunities. This specialized training would benefit both the lawyer, the firm and the markets that they serve."

The Champion thought about it for a minute and said, *"Let me check in with my existing people and see if they have any specialised programming for women. If they do, then I will stick with them; if they don't, I'll look to recommend you guys if the opportunity arises."*

Within a month, that new Champion referred the first firm to us. Once we got into that firm working with female lawyers, we started to get male lawyers asking for coaching as well and took over a majority of the business. Because the client was seeing measurable results and reporting it back to the Champion, who referred us, we were able to secure an equal footing over time with our competitor. Referrals were handed out regularly and equally, but with us getting ALL the referrals to firms looking to launch female initiatives. We didn't displace our competition; we simply took a share of the opportunity, and the Champion became 'conditioned 'to ask law firms if they struggled with keeping their female lawyers and promoting them to the partnership ranks.

This strategy unearthed excellent opportunities for us to establish our position with the female lawyer market, and we got 50% of the male lawyer market as a byproduct of our efforts.

"I don't know if giving out your information is fair to others."

This objection reflects someone who wants to be seen as neutral to everyone for fear of losing opportunities themselves (Switzerland). They may have missed opportunities themselves in the past for playing 'favourites' or had some other repercussions or accusations of being unfair to everyone.

I see this most in novice professionals. Established professionals are past the point of political sensitivities around referring/supporting others, and simply look for the best person to promote as the best solution.

Here's how to respond:

"I appreciate that in some situations, it may not be appropriate to hand one name to a prospect as certain parts of the market may see this as favouritism. I wonder if a better tact might be to accumulate three names of companies doing what we do within this niche market and asking each of them to furnish you with what they do specifically for that market.

When an opportunity arises, you can share the three different solutions and allow the prospective client to determine which meets their needs best. That way, you are just shortlisting a group of potential providers, and the onus lies on the prospect to determine which firm best suits their needs.

You aren't saying one is better than the other. You are just sharing how they differ in approach or service provision. The prospect sees you as making their work easier to find a solution; the companies you are mentioning get an opportunity to showcase their solution, and you are seen as pointing the prospect in the right direction rather than at a particular vender.

Would that be something that could work? A simple way to put this into play is to have a handful of vendors in this niche tell you:

What they do···

Why it matters···

Who cares...

The responsibility lies on the vendors to make it easy for you to share this information with a prospect. You, as the Champion, aren't required to compare and contrast the services. "

Most Champions will go for this as it gives them an excuse if a vendor complains of unfair attention given to a vendor. They can say, *"I'm open to learning about what all businesses do so that when a person/company needs a solution, I can offer a handful of companies that I know offer that solution. Then the person/company can explore for themselves, which one makes the most sense for them at that time."*

"I'm trying to wind things down. I don't want more responsibility."

This objection is most prevalent with someone nearing the end of their career. They could also be overwhelmed with what they have on their plate and thinking you are only adding more to an already busy schedule. The best way to address this objection is to showcase how Champions are more 'observers 'than 'active hunters '(even though we love active hunters who are bringing in prospects regularly).

Share the fact that them being your Champion is just something that can be done when the opportunity arises and without them having to go out of their way. They do this in the course of their regular day — no additional efforts required.

Here's how to respond:

"I know you are trying to slow things down/have a lot on your plate. Let me explain what this might look like as it takes no real additional effort on your part. My job is to let you know what I do, why it matters, and who it matters to. Throughout your regular day, you aren't doing anything extraordinary for me. No additional time. No additional effort. You are just mindful of what I do, whom I do it for, and why people want it. Within your ordinary day, if you hear someone looking for what we do or having a problem that is within our wheelhouse, you offer to share our information (if you

have no time) or make an email introduction (if you have 3 minutes to spare).

In exchange for just keeping me in front of mind, you gain me as a Champion for you. You let me know what you need or where I can offer you value, and I go about my day, doing regular activities and look to support you when something floats right by me. I see something that I know you need, I drop you an email or pick up the phone and let you know. It won't take much of my time either by we can support each other as we go through our day. You may have months of not seeing anything for me and then see three opportunities in a week. I'd like you and me to explore becoming Champions for each other, but we can go slow. Opportunities will come when they come."

This usually is enough to get the person engaged and then your job is to do the first Champion activity for them. As always, we model the behaviour.

Here's an example of how this goes into play.

I had a Champion who worked at a commercial bank. They were doing the job of two people and busy as hell. They had more to deal with than they could handle and didn't want to take on any additional responsibilities.

I said to her, "I understand. I'd like to be your Champion and for you to be mine. How about this. When you are doing your reviews with your corporate clients, if you notice their sales are going in the wrong direction and you hear from them they need help getting their sales up, you offer to get them 30 minutes with us in person or by phone to suggest some ways to get sales growth in place.

This is a value add you will offer your clients that we will not bill them for. It allows us to get in front of a prospective client, and we will leave them better than we found them.

We will not hard sell them (not our style) and will give them a tool or two they can start to use whether they work with us or not. This would all be suggested during the review you are doing anyways, and the onus is on your client to book a time to talk with us if they want.

Whether they do or don't is not of importance to you. You get the brownie points for making the offer. On the other side, you keep me updated with what you need personally. Do you need to meet someone specific? Are you struggling with something in business that I can help with? Need a new assistant? You call or email me to let me know, and I'll see what

I can do to get a solution in place for you or at least point you in the right direction.

Neither of us needs to go out of our way. We benefit from using the other as a potential solution to a problem right in front of us. Is that something you'd like to explore with me?"

She said, *"Yes...we can try it, but I don't want you to have high expectations of me."*

I said, *"I won't, but I want to be your first call when you need something and in regards to your clients. If you have a sales question that comes up during a session, feel free to call or email me, and I'll try to answer it for you. I want to become your #1 Sales Resource."*

Not only did she become a Champion, she ended up becoming a coaching client as well.

"I'm precluded from being able to make recommendations (lawyer/government/etc.)."

Some professionals have mandates to not show preference of one vendor over another (government), while others practice this as a rule to mitigate any suggested risk or conflict of interest that might arise from such a recommendation (some lawyers).

These people can still be valuable to you, especially if they tick many of the boxes that we use to assess potential Champions (extroverted, respected, established in the niche market, etc.).

Many can be very powerful to align with and source information from. Not in the form of inside information (which again can break some ethical responsibilities), but in the form of their 'opinion 'on things. And they can be a great gateway to other

Champions that are in a position to talk about you to others and make introductions.

Here's how to respond:

"I appreciate that you are unable to show preference from one vendor to another given your position. I wonder if we could do things a little bit differently. I highly respect your opinion on things.

From time to time, I'd like to check in with you and weigh your opinion on things (what markets are doing, the viability of ideas, how things might sound that I'm using in my presentation, and so on) — just more of a sounding board to what I'm doing from someone I respect.

As well, as I'm approaching other gatekeepers in these markets, I'd like to be able to inquire with you if you think that my time is best invested there or that I might benefit from focusing elsewhere.

In asking you to be my Champion in this format, I'd want to understand how to best champion or support your initiatives, so I'd like to spend some time on what you currently have on your plate that I might offer some support on."

*These types of prospective Champions can be harder to engage but are well worth the effort. Even if they don't fully activate for you, your relationship with them will hold cache when at events where others can see you have access to them. I've found in the political world, mayors are terrible Champions in regards to introducing me to people remotely, yet at events, they will happily walk around with me and connect me to their contacts in the room.

This situation is one of those rare occasions where you want to be flexible with how you use a Champion and not put a square peg in a round hole.

Example:

I have a client who oversees a Merger & Acquisitions practice at a top ten law firm. He has never acknowledged my role as his business coach and never referred a client to me directly. Yet, when we attend conferences together, he sits with me the whole time, invites contacts to sit and drink with us, and acknowledges that his 'firm' has hired us to do business development training for their senior associates.

Because of how well respected he is in law circles, just being in his vicinity raises my profile to potential clients. Because he acknowledges that 'they' work with us, we establish both visibility and credibility immediately. While he would never say, *"you should call Ghost CEO,"* his contacts almost always ask for a business card, and they would *"like to hear more about what we do."*

Needless to say, when he is attending a legal conference or giving a speech at one, I do my best to ensure I'm in attendance.

"I don't know if I'm comfortable doing that yet."

Even if the objection isn't verbalized like this, you'll pick up through body language that you are asking too soon, or rushing it. It might be just a bit too early in the relationship for them, BUT I don't want that to stop you. Some Champions are ready to go right away (especially if you have your Three Questions sorted AND they don't have a current solution for what you offer).

Others need a bit of time to feel comfortable knowing that their relationship and reputation hinges on the recommendations they make to others. I like it when people are cautious. When they do Champion, it will hold much more weight with their markets.

Here's how to respond:

"I appreciate that we may need to develop our relationship a bit more before you feel comfortable being my Champion. I see this as a long term, mutually beneficial relationship and certainly worth the investment for me.

When you champion others, what do you need to have seen first to have absolute comfort in recommending /championing them?

Is there a first step that we can take that will showcase to you that I can deliver and allow you to observe that I am who I appear to be?

Is there someone that it might make sense for you to talk with that give their perspective on what working with me looks like (you would likely use another Champion to accomplish this)?

Let's figure out a step by step approach that isn't rushed so that you feel comfortable, and in the meantime, I can begin to Champion you. I'm in this for a long term relationship, so I don't want to rush anything and always ensure that we both feel comfortable."

"I think you should do it on your own."

This answer is a 'dust off' and usually suggests that they don't want to Champion you for whatever reason.

- Maybe they have someone else.

- Maybe they don't like or trust you.

- Maybe they think you have a crappy reputation or don't do good work.

- Sometimes they may think you too junior for them to champion and want you to get experience before they are prepared to put their name on you.

Whatever the reason, they are trying to shut it down for now.

Do not let this objection cloud your view of Champions or your value. Some people have been burned by people before and are gun shy. Some people don't want others to be more successful than them. Some didn't have Champions (because they didn't know the strategy) and don't want to see anyone else do it better/faster/stronger than they did. In most cases, assuming it isn't a reputation or experience issue on your part, it is more about them than you.

Here's how to respond:

"I am doing the work as well, but I believe in building mutually beneficial relationships with leaders in my niche markets. This isn't about us going out of our way or adding things to our already busy plates. Instead, it's about keeping an eye out for each other for when opportunities present themselves. You seem like someone I could Champion, and I was hoping to be the same for you. But if you don't think it's a fit, we can put a pin in it for now and maybe revisit it in the future if something changes. Is there anything you'd need to see from me to make it an easy decision to become an active Champion? If you have any ideas on how I could become a valuable Champion for you, let's pick up the conversation."

Remember that 'no 'often means 'not right now, 'so you are curious to see what might need to be in place to shift their thinking and also what they may be looking for in a Champion for themselves.

We are trying to uncover what their issue is without coming right out and asking them. Then we keep an active eye on it. Truthfully, there are too many prospective Champions out there to lose sleep or invest too much time over these rare creatures. Don't do anything for them until you see an adjustment in their openness to work with you.

"I wouldn't know where to start."

Read this objection instead, as "I'd need you to tell me what I would need to do clearly." This is a chance to start them off slow and get them some 'wins ' as a Champion and also for them to get used to you being their Champion.

Remove discretion (don't make them have to think about what to do), give a clear explanation (markets you serve, the solution you provide, what to say to others), and model the behaviour (be the Champion you want in your business). Doing these three things and your Champions will be set up for success.

Here's how to respond.

"We'd keep it super simple. I'd like you to keep an eye out for opportunities that I may be able to offer a solution for. And an eye out for other professionals that I should meet. Just that. Every once in a while, when your schedule allows, I may sneak you out for lunch (my treat) and pick your brain on things you are noticing in the market or get your opinion on something.

The only things to do right now are:

1) Me to explain what I do, what it matters, and who most cares.

2) *Explain what makes me/us the ideal solution for our niche market and what a perfect client looks like for us.*

3) *Me to be very clear on how I can be a Champion for you and what I might be able to do for you immediately.*

It's just that simple. I'll go to work on doing Champion activities for you, and you become familiar with the types of clients we work with, and if one comes across your path and you think we could add value, you offer to introduce us. That's it aside from me treating you to lunch periodically when you are free."

*There are many other things you can get them to do, but start small and manageable. You don't want this to feel like a burden for them, and you want them to get a taste of you being their Champion as soon as possible, so they see that they selfishly benefit by having you active. In turn, they will want to become active as well to keep you engaged.

"I don't want to disappoint you."

This statement means one of two things:

1) I don't know if I can do what you want me to.

2) I don't ever do what I say I'm going to, so best not to ask me.

If the former, we can work on that with clarity of what we need from that specific Champion.

If the latter, we will find that out sooner than later, but in either case, best to proceed with the right intentions and observe to see which it is.

Here's how to respond:

"I wouldn't ask you if I thought you would disappoint me. All I want is:

To become an excellent Champion for you in which I will model the behaviour of what I'm looking for by example.

It is my responsibility to share with you what we do, why it matters, and who cares (ideal clients) and your job to work with me in understanding how to be a great Champion for you.

It will happen over time if we keep it in mind, but the great thing is we do this through the course of our typical day. We don't have to step outside the lines or add additional work to our plate. Your job as my Champion is not to get me clients. Your role is to see an opportunity, and if appropriate, bring my name up and offer an introduction, or just bring it to my attention."

*When you look at it like this, you are taking all the guesswork out of their Champion role. If you were taking them fishing, you are loading the boat, putting it in the water, baiting their hook, casting it, and then handing the rod over to them to hold in one hand while they drink a beer in the other, that you brought, chilled, and opened for them. You do the work, so your Champions only have to watch for opportunities going by in front of them. Simple.

With that said, our section on objections is complete. Are there others that aren't listed here? Possibly.

If you come across one, feel free to email us, and we'll do our best to answer it for you and add it to a future version of this book. You can reach us at: champions@ghostceo.com

I'm hopeful that you feel prepared for what might come up. More in your head what you can deal with now, but if others show any version of the objection, address it with directness, compassion, and conciseness. We are not convincing anyone of anything. We are looking to add value and get value from people we know and appreciate in our business circles. Business is a team sport. We are looking for the right teammates. That's all. They either want to play, or they don't — no wrong answers.

That's all the 'content 'that is required to launch a Champion strategy. Now in the last few chapters, we move to 'context'...how to put this content into practice. From becoming an exceptional Champion yourself (we need to model the behaviour), to having the actual talk (step by step process), and finally, how to take care of those precious Champions once we have them activated.

Chapter 6:

First things first: Becoming a model Champion yourself

Business is full of hypocrisy. There's no shortage of people quick to tell you what to do but not doing it themselves. Finding someone who 'walks their walk' is an exception to the rule rather than the rule itself. We (you and me) must model the behaviours that we want from others. We become the yardstick that others measure themselves against to manage expectations. We don't drop to the level of the market; we encourage the market to rise to the level we set. We don't ask for favours and then offer one in return. We go first. Once we have done our part, then we ask them for their part. We are easy to Champion because we are clear, concise, focused, disciplined, and systemized. Everything we do can be described by these words if we hope to have a full stable of Champions we support and whose support we can both count on and measure.

At this point in the book, you now know the transformative impact Champions can have on your business and bottom line. You learn a lot about attracting and keeping Champions by being a great Champion yourself. They say the best way to get an adult learner to embrace education is to let them know they are going to have to teach it to others. It changes the mindset. And assuming that most of your Champions may not have had previous access to this book, you are going to be 'coaching' them through the process. If you only remember one thing from this chapter, make it this:

It only takes 10% of the effort to keep a Champion as it does to find a Champion.

Every time you identify and activate a Champion but don't play your role correctly, you lose not only all the time you invested in getting them on-boarded, you also lose all future opportunities they could have created for you.

Most mistakes with Champion management can be traced back to one fundamental challenge on your part...you are not being an excellent Champion for them and not modelling the behaviours.

Accepting this as fact, the power we yield is in our actions and efforts to become the absolute best Champion for our circle. Consider this chapter your quick 'Bootcamp' to Champion Excellence.

You will become the model for your Champions to become their best versions that they can be (to your selfish benefit). You are the guinea pig of your model. By doing the work first (just like answering the Three Questions), you have experience in how to become a Champion and can thus train Champions more effectively.

What does it take to become a good Champion?

There are many components to becoming a great Champion. The first and most important being, 'intention.' You intend to become an exceptional Champion to your network. Someone who can be trusted, leveraged, who keeps an eye out for others, speaks to solutions, makes introductions, and follows up. You do this by developing the skills we use in the report card, assessing our own Champions. We become what we seek.

- We influence niche market(s).

- We have an established network of contacts.

- We have a solid reputation.

- We are extroverted (or if introverted, have ways of connecting people in a way that is both effective and comfortable for us).

- We are articulate and can learn answers to the Three Questions for others.

- We are active in their markets.

- We have an established relationship with the people we Champion.

- We can be championed by others effectively.

When I'm practicing being the best version of a Champion possible, I always put myself in the role of someone running for mayor. I shake hands, kiss babies, and collect people into my network.

Every person I meet gets categorized in my mind:

- Client

- Prospective client

- Prospective client for one of my clients/colleagues

- Strategic partner for me or one of my clients/colleagues

- Prospective Champion for me or one of my clients/colleagues

- Random contact to keep in my network and try to develop later

- Someone who I'm unable to determine their value at this time (professionally)

As a goal, I look to increase my professional network by at least 80 'valuable' people per month.

Doing so gives me many contacts to leverage for my markets and connections.

I think of it like a baseball card collection. I have cards to trade with others to have a complete set. I may pick up cards that are not necessarily good for my business model, but useful for those I do business with. I go out of my way to make those connections for my network. I sincerely love being in a room with 20 people and noticing that most, if not all, the relationships can be derived from my work introducing them, or them introducing one another after me making the initial connection.

The many hats of a Champion.

Because I know there is more than one type of Champion, I look to build my skills in all versions/functions of being a Champions.

The primary function I bring to the table is to 'bird dog' opportunities, for those I champion, with prospective clients.

Bird dogging:

The process of shaking the trees for prospects. Similar to a hunting dog who runs into the bush to move birds or prey out so they can be hunted.

Recently I was meeting with a prospect who I realized, five minutes into the meeting, was too small for our business model. So I turned off my sales hat and put on my Champion hat. Who did I know who could benefit from this person or who could benefit this person? It came out that the person I was meeting was unhappy with his current accountant. It just so happens I have a local accountant that I Champion.

I told him, "Listen, I don't think our business coaching model is right for you at the moment, but I do think we can offer a solution to your accounting issue. A good friend of mine owns an established accounting practice here in town and will be able to offer you sound advice on many of the decisions that you are making right now. He acts as a CFO to established business owners and ensures you have all the relevant financial information to make great strategic decisions. I'll introduce you by email today, and he will see you as soon as your schedule allows because it is coming from me. Then when you grow your business up to $500K, circle back around with me and let's explore doing some business together."

The prospect was very happy I had an accounting solution for him and considered the introduction a considerable favour.

The accountant felt I had sourced a great prospective client for him and one that understood his strategic value rather than just overseeing the books and doing year-end returns. They ended up engaging in a business relationship and are enjoying working together. The one introduction I made between the two of them got me two points — one from our future client and one from the existing accountant whom I Champion. I didn't go out of my way to source that client for him. I simply came across the opportunity within my typical day of business and made the connection. Now both feel like they 'owe' me one. I like that. It can be that easy. I'm selfish, and I'm selfless. I look for what benefits me first and others second. If there isn't a benefit for me, I don't abandon it. I look for how I can leverage goodwill moving forward. It's intentional.

In another example, I was meeting with a realtor in Boston, again prospecting them. At about the 15-minute mark, I determined that our model wouldn't work with their team dynamic but continued to press them on how their model worked and their niche markets.

In conversation, I found out that she struggled with people coming to look at houses but not being pre-approved for a mortgage yet.

To illustrate the importance of Champions to this realtor, I asked her if she'd like to hear about a solution I would use if I were her.

She said she would, and I said, "I know a mortgage broker in town who co-hosts open houses with realtors. She has the technological ability to approve people on the spot and could qualify potential buyers while they are visiting your open house. That way, you know if they are real prospects, and if not, you would know what level they would pre-qualify at and look at the inventory that might fit that level and sell them into that."

She got a big grin on her face and said, "I would very much like the opportunity to meet that mortgage broker."

I told her, "I'm happy to Champion you and make that introduction, but I would also like to keep the conversation going about you becoming a Champion for us to your self-employed clients with established businesses and over $1M in revenue. We'd very much like to meet those clients when appropriate". She agreed.

After the meeting, I hopped in the car and called the mortgage broker (who happened to be a current client and Champion of our firm) and said, "I just met one of the top real estate brokers in Boston. While not a prospect for us, she is going to Champion us into her self-employed clients with established businesses. She was very interested when I brought you up and your willingness to co-host open houses and pre-qualify buyers. She particularly liked the part of knowing what they are qualifying at so that she can sell them into another home if that's an option. This could open up a whole new clientele for you. I'm going to make that introduction for you because I'm your Champion. While you are doing business with her, I want you to also keep an eye out for those established, self-employed professionals who you might be able to introduce us to if the opportunity arises."

The mortgage broker emphatically agreed and thanked me over and over again.

Let's unpack this example. I found out what one person's challenge was. I had a solution in my network that could solve that problem, and I was able to articulate it to the realtor. I then called the mortgage broker, preparing her for the opportunity. I also got commitments from both to 'bird dog' for us. Two professionals, sharing one introduction, felt like they 'owed' me a favour.

1 Introduction = 2 favours. Nice.

I can call either of them at any time, and ask for any introduction I want. They will do it immediately because I have become both 'valuable' and necessary. They want me to be happy and to continue doing what makes them happy (referrals). This is Human Psychology 101.

I'm using these examples to illustrate for you, the practice of being a great Champion.

Let's shift gears a bit.

I have a colleague that offers a complimentary service to what we do. He's not coachable (long story) but is valuable to the clients and businesses he serves.

Even though I've disqualified him as a prospective client for us, in his work, he serves potential clients for us. He is quick to introduce us when his clients are having sales/business development issues.

He decided that he was going to start hunting for accounting firms (of which we have substantial experience and clientele). He invited me for lunch to find out the best way to approach an accounting firm and establish a long-term relationship with them.

In this situation, my role as Champion was to share with him best practices and act as a sounding board for his sales ideas. I wasn't able to make introductions for him (as I usually would) because he is opening up a geographical market that we aren't in. But by me giving him insight into the process of identifying and engaging firms of this nature, I saved him years of experimentation to find out what works. He knows he can tap into my knowledge, and he also knows that my availability to him is in direct relation to the way he Champions my firm and me. It needs to be fair. Not necessarily one for one, but value for value.

Be generous with your network connecting 'like with like.'

Just like the coach of a sports team, you will have your top players (starters), your clutch players (mid-level) and your grinders (the proven foot soldiers) in your network. It's essential to match 'like with like.' You do this by matching people of the same level and strategic importance to you.

I don't put the head of a global hedge fund with a relatively new lawyer with five years of experience.

I don't put a 'killer sales person' with someone figuring out how to clearly describe what they do.

I match people of the same calibre with one another, which requires me to sort them by type.

Here are the questions I go through in my head for each person as I inventory them to figure out where they go in my network and who is of my value to them and whom they can offer the most value to.

- How long have they been in business?

- What is the level of business they are most comfortable with? Are they advanced, moderate, beginner?

- Who is their ideal client type?

- What types of contacts are of most value to them right now?

- What people would be most interested in meeting this person?

- How important of a contact is this person in my network?

- Is this person a strong Champion of mine and do they introduce me to key people?

- How many opportunities has this person generated for me in the last six months, and what's the value (quantitative and qualitative) to my business model?

You may read this list (and others in the book) and think that I'm impersonal or transactional with how I sort people, but nothing could be farther from the truth. I respect the time of everyone I'm engaged with. I look to create enormous value for my network. I am at my best when I'm organised and know what players I have on the board and who would work well with whom. I quickly determine who gets how much of my time and how I'm going to invest that time. Some people get an email from me. Some get a phone call. Some get in-person visits when I can make it work.

And a few get my time whenever they need it. These are usually my clients and my top-performing Champions.

Some people may refer a client a month to us, which is valuable to me. Others may refer one opportunity a year, but that opportunity could be worth 100 clients. Comparing the two, the second has a more significant, measurable value to me. I would spend even more time on understanding how to be an exceptional Champion for the latter than the former, even though both bring me business. It's all about time management and return on my time investment.

I don't assign my time or effort on people's potential but instead on their performance. Within the first 90 seconds of meeting a person, I can determine if my network can benefit from knowing them and they from knowing my network Within 90 minutes I know if they can be a Champion and if I can Champion them. Within 90 days of knowing them, I know if they are worth long term effort or if I should let them die on the vine. If at the 90–day mark I'm undecided than

I usually default to it being a 'no' for putting in additional effort.

But I always start with being generous with my market and new contacts. If a new connection needs something, I may give them one of my mid-tier contacts or solutions to see how they do with that. If they do a good job and it becomes something mutually beneficial (good for the two parties I introduced), I may connect them with additional contacts assuming that they are doing the same for me. We always pay it forward and go first on the 'good deed' train. If, after the first connection, I don't see some level of reciprocation, I will check in to make sure that they understand what we do, why it matters, and who cares.

If I'm satisfied that they know how to represent us and just aren't noticing anything, I'll give it a bit more time (but no additional resources or time investment) and see if we get any bites.

At the end of the 90 days, I pull the stakes up and move on (basically leave that prospective Champion out in the cold.) If I do see movement and reciprocity, I will make more introductions being mindful not to get too far ahead of them but to match the value. If they offer me a whale of an opportunity, I may make 4–5 separate introductions for them, to match the value.

This is a great situation to be in when you are playing 'catch up' because your Champions are giving you such valuable connections.

Overall, I want my network to know that I have a large and growing contact list, and I'm happy to share it, but I need to see it going both ways. If not, I close the address book and put another player on the field.

Don't waste peoples' time.

One big challenge when connecting people with one another, whether it be a vendor to a client or contact to contact, is making sure I'm not wasting anyone's time. Both parties need to know that I see a reason for them becoming connected and that it makes sense to schedule time with one another (either by phone or in-person). I don't make introductions just to make introductions. I make introductions that make sense for both people and add value. If I don't, points aren't earned; they are deducted.

Look for the win/win with all connections.

Building on the previous point, I don't leave the reason for the meeting up in the air or for them to figure out among themselves. I regularly use email to introduce people to one another, only after I've talked to both parties (generally by phone) and outlined why I think they need to meet each other.

Then in the email, I recap why I think the introduction makes sense and what the opportunity(s) are from the connection that are worth exploring.

Going back to the mortgage broker/realtor example we previously discussed. I talked with both sides about how the other could benefit their business model. Then I made the email introduction laying out the value to both (which I knew they already knew because I'd talked to them individually) and then invited them to connect 'when schedules allow' and see what comes of it.

After emails like this, I ask both parties to keep me updated with what happens for a couple of reasons:

- I want to know how they show up when I introduce them to others.

- I want to know that they understood the reason for the connection and honoured its value.

- I want to see them move the opportunity forward and not just meet to meet and not take action from it.

- I want to see how long they take to connect, which gives me insight into how serious they take introductions that I make. If it takes you a week to respond to a connection I make, I'm certainly not going to introduce you to a prospective client/contact that I know appreciates quick turnaround.

*One of the other things I like to notice is how quickly people realize the opportunity that is being offered to them when I suggest the connection. Do they see it immediately or do I need to lay it out for them?

People will say, "why do I want to meet with this person?" At this point, I explain the value to them and how I expect them to offer value to the other person I'm connecting them to.

I'm okay explaining this once or twice, but by the third time, I want them to begin to see the opportunities for themselves, or at least have faith that I don't waste their time with useless connections.

If, after 2–3 introductions, I need to keep on laying out why these meetings are essential, I usually put a pin in the person not grasping it and move on to someone else. They are making it hard for me to be their Champion, and unless they are a unicorn Champion for me, I look for more simple ways to do business. Additionally, if I'm making introductions and they aren't converting the opportunity, I also sideline them and move on to someone who can close the deal when it's presented. It isn't emotional. It's just business.

If something is one-sided, admit it and offer a voucher.

There are situations, albeit infrequent, where I want to introduce two people for the sole benefit of only one of them. Maybe I have a client who wants to shoot a tv show and a contact who is a television producer. The benefit is obvious to the client who needs to know the inner workings of the television world and less to the producer who may not be interested in the show, given the genre they work in. I'm well aware that I need to leverage a 'favour' to make this happen, but because I'm quick to offer favours to my inner circle, I have some in the bank.

I play it like this:

To the client:

"I'm going to attempt to get you a meeting with one of my guys who is a television producer with a tonne of credits under his belt. Your show is outside his genre but he will meet with you if I ask him. Get all your questions ready and take him to a nice restaurant for lunch. You'll have an hour, so prioritize your questions from most important to least important."

To my colleague, who is a producer:

"I have a client with a television show that needs some insight into how these broadcast deals work. It's outside of your genre, but she's a huge Champion and could be valuable to you later on. Because I'm unsure of the value to you but clear on your value to her, would you do this for me as a favour knowing that you have an IOU with me whenever you want to use it?"

He agreed, knowing I'm always good to return the favour. I made the email introduction. They met, and she got a tremendous amount out of the meeting.

I was her Champion. He was my Champion. He knows that I'm available to Champion him whenever he needs it.

This was a rare, one-sided situation, but it worked because everyone got something. I got the client access; the client got access; my colleague has an IOU from me he can use whenever he wants. Always look for ways to make things work, and as your reputation grows, favours become even more comfortable to grant and ask for.

Be on the lookout for all opportunities and then who should have them (Easter Egg Hunt).

What I like most about collecting people and activating Champions/becoming a Champion for them, is that it reminds me of an Easter Egg Hunt. Every person I meet, an event I attend, or newspaper I read, is full of opportunities. I am bombarded with chances to be a great Champion/connector/leader. I love fielding all these opportunities and considering who should receive them from me.

When I meet a star Commercial Banker, I go through my list of contacts in my mind and decide:

- Who needs a good Commercial Banker now?

- Who would benefit from knowing this banker?

- Who would be interested in getting on this banker's radar screen?

- What people do I know that this Commercial Banker would like to meet?

- Who could I connect this banker with where they could build business together (alliance)?

- Who could I connect this banker with where they could do business with each other?

- Whom do I know who could get business opportunities from this banker?

It is SUPER rare for me to meet someone and not know whom I could connect them with or who they should be connected to. It's almost a sport for me now because I've been doing it for so long.

My greatest challenge isn't identifying the opportunities, but instead, pumping the brakes and determining what types of opportunities I want to give to who. I tend to focus more on individuals that hustle than those who sit back and wait for things to happen.

If I have something of value but I know my Champions won't be interested in it, I will throw it to a second-tier contact to see what they do with it and if they reciprocate.

Sometimes it's personal. So be it.

There will be times when the people I'm championing might need something personal rather than professional. Tickets to an event, a letter of endorsement for their kid applying to school, even an unattainable bottle of whisky for one of their top clients. I pride myself on trying to become people's first call when they are stuck on something. I don't know how to solve everything, but I do have a list of contacts that afford me almost superhuman abilities (benefit of collecting smart, established people in my networks).

For those that I champion, it can be me planting a seed in the mind of one of their target prospects that I know. It can be giving them insight into the cities they are travelling into and how to navigate them. Recently I was able to get someone I champion a very 'hard to get' reservation at a restaurant in New York through another Champion who is friends with the Chef. I love this because this is the dinner party story, to be told many times in the future, that let others know about me making something happen. It isn't ego; it's pride that I can make things happen for those that are so generous to me. I'm thrilled to reciprocate.

If I introduce you to a good Investment Banker, that doesn't get shared in polite small talk at your PTA meeting. But if I get you a signed cookbook by a celebrity chef, and you are bragging to your foodie friends about it, my name will likely come up in the story. Then the story turns to, 'how did HE make it happen?" The answer is something like, "I'm not sure. It arrived on my birthday."

I want to be that unicorn in peoples' stories.

Even though I like my Champions to focus their support of me through the lens of business, I'm certainly happy to champion others both professionally or personally, especially if they are strategically valuable to me. If it can be done and they need it done, I'll find a way to get it done.

Sometimes you need to be a Ghost Champion for your Champions' Champions.

That's a mouthful. This is a more advanced application of championing and something I wasn't even going to add because we haven't even got to how to have the 'Champion conversation' yet.

Let alone the proper 'handling and feeding' of your Champions.

But I'm going to stick it here because it has come up three times this week. I'd invite you to skim over this part, dog-ear the corner of this page, and come back to after you have your first ten Champions activated.

One thing you can do for your Champions is helping them be great Champions to their Champions. Sound like a Zen riddle?

Let's unpack:

You have a Champion who is struggling to support one of their Champions with something they need. They don't have the know-how, the network, or the solution their Champion currently needs. So they come to you (or you offer) to pinch-hit the situation for them. The person receiving the favour need not know of your involvement as you are doing this for your Champion, not theirs.

Example:

Eric has a Champion who throws him a lot of business. His Champion is a huge Seattle Seahawks fan, and he'd like to do something but doesn't know what to do (Eric doesn't like football that much) and doesn't even know where to start. But he knows he wants to do something special to acknowledge how much his Champion has contributed to his business.

Eric knows that if he ever gets stuck on doing something memorable for a Champion, he need just reach out to me, and we can brainstorm what to do (because I'm also a Champion of Eric and introduced him to the strategy).

So he reaches out with the situation, and I say, "Why don't you find out what game your Champion is going to and we can get him down on the field after the game?" Eric is excited by this because he knows it will blow his Champion's mind. Here's our process:

1) He finds out which game his Champion is going to.

2) I get the inside details from someone in my network on how to get a group down on the field.

3) I give Eric the details on how to set it up.

4) He calls and sets it up.

5) Champion's mind is blown (and the three other people the Champion is attending the game with).

6) Champion continues to refer work to Eric because he feels appreciated and wants to reciprocate.

One of the three people also attending the game starts working with Eric, which is a beautiful byproduct of being a good Champion.

So in review:

I championed my Champion by helping him champion his Champion. Now Eric is looking for ways to show his appreciation to me for making him look good.

Make sense?

As you become a well-versed and practiced Champion of others, your value goes through the roof. By mastering this strategy, you become the go-to person for people and inadvertently can become the builder of other peoples' Champions groups. Eric's Champion never knew I was involved, and I was happy to play the role of King Maker rather than King. Arguably the most influential role of all.

*Remember to 'dog ear' this page and revisit it after you have been building Champions for a while. You'll see the power of it and appreciate how much it endears you to your Champions being their 'first call.'

Chapter 7:

The Process of Activating a Champion

It's meeting time! You now know:

- What a Champion is

- What a Champion does

- The different roles Champions play in our business

- How to become an easy person to champion

- How to identify and grade potential Champions

- How we become a dominant Champion ourselves

- How to address all objections.

We are ready to have our initial Champion conversations. Prepare yourself to stumble a bit in the beginning. It's all part of the process. I want you to take your list of twenty prospective Champions and approach them in reverse order from least valuable to most valuable.

Or you can order them from most forgiving to least forgiving. Family members and friends make perfect tackling dummies to role-play this process with. This will allow you a warm body to talk with and get into the flow of the conversation.

Invest time in this process of applying your new-found knowledge and putting it to work. Do not rush it. The process is as important as the outcome. You want to make sure all the prospective Champions you approach are people that will represent you well and that you can be an exceptional Champion for in return.

Friendly reminder:

Don't stray too far off this process in the beginning. Every day we have clients trying to customize this strategy without practicing it in its pure form. When it doesn't create the opportunities they expect, they are mystified way. It's because they are messing with the recipe. Or worse, they start onboarding the wrong types of Champions, which is equally tragic.

This process will produce results if you follow it correctly. Later on, as you become more comfortable with this strategy and have executed it 40 or 50x, then you have my full permission to play with it a bit, but I want you to master the fundamentals first. If, for whatever reason, what you are trying isn't working, you can return to the fundamentals.

Also, if at any point in the future your Champion strategy feels like it is losing speed or going stale, pick up this book, read through it again, and figure out where you might be off the path.

Now a couple of pieces of housekeeping before getting into the recipe.

Face to Face

"Can I make the 'ask 'over the phone or by email?" This is a question I get all the time from clients who like to rush through things to get them done and checked off their list.

The quick answer is **no**. This conversation is an important 'ask 'and best done in an intimate, face to face, situation.

If geography prohibits you from meeting face to face, then I would suggest a video conference (Skype, FaceTime, etc.) so that you can have a slightly deeper connection than just by phone and see each others' faces.

If video is not available, or if the prospective Champion isn't comfortable or familiar with video (a more likely possibility with mature Champions), then the phone is the worst-case scenario but still better than not actioning them at all.

Never use email to activate a Champion. Email can be used later to manage Champions, but only AFTER the relationship has been established.

So in preferential order:

1) In person meeting

2) Video conference (what I call a virtual coffee chat)

3) Telephone call

4) NEVER email. NEVER!

There should be more than enough Champions in your physical vicinity to make this work and get you started, especially with our first milestone of 10 Champions.

As a quick reminder:

1–6 months we want you to attract your first ten active Champions

6–12 continue to manage those ten Champions

12–18 months we get up to twenty-five Champions

18+ months we move towards having fifty active Champions.

We don't ever go over 50 Champions as the number becomes unmanageable. If we want to add a new Champion to our list, we drop the worst performing Champion off our list (what we refer to as 'drafting'). Only so many seats on the bus, so don't exceed the fire limit.

Breaking Bread

I like to conduct my Champion on-boarding meeting over lunch or breakfast. Coffee is okay in a pinch. Dinner is okay too, but if alcohol is involved, you may be required to explain things over again after the meeting.

The process of breaking bread with someone creates intimacy as we spend most of our meals with family and friends, so it sets a tone. When possible, invite them to breakfast or lunch, somewhere nice (and quiet), where you would typically host someone important that brings you a client a month (the expectations of our Champions when they are warmed up).

Choose somewhere where you won't be disturbed by people you know or background noise. Somewhere you can have a clear and open conversation. I like to have late breakfasts or late lunches, which allow me to avoid most distractions — breakfast at 930AM; lunch at 130PM. You will have to navigate what works best for your schedule and that of your Champion.

There is nothing worse than trying to have the Champion conversation while being interrupted by noise from other tables, concern about others listening in, or people coming up to your table to say hello to you or your guest. It ruins the flow of the conversation.

You could also meet in either of your offices, but I've found this to be problematic with phone calls, people knocking on the door with a 'quick question, ' et cetera. You want this conversation to go through without interruption. Manage the environment as best as you can.

Another option to consider is going for a walk with your prospective Champion. I like to go for long walks when the weather holds and will regularly invite Champion prospects to walk with me if I know they are into it. I grab us coffees (my first opportunity to find out what they like to drink for future visits/meetings) and go for a stroll with them for an hour or so.

This approach works very well for me and may for you too once you know your process of having a conversation with a Champion — lots of different ways to build on this theme. If you are a sailor, maybe you invite them out on your boat. If you are a gardener, invite them over to have a coffee in your backyard. A golfer might take them out for a round. It's entirely up to you to figure out what environment will work best for these conversations. I've even had them carpooling to an event or in a lounge at a conference. This is where you can customise the strategy to your liking as long as what you choose offers you a chance to have a full and uninterrupted conversation.

NOTE: In the beginning, you may want to keep it to a restaurant or yours/their office so that you can bullet point the following process, but once you've done it a dozen times or so, you're probably ready to do it outside or during another activity.

Now let's get into the recipe of having the conversation

Step 1: Making the invitation

Choose the prospective Champion you'd like to activate and extend the invitation to connect. Let on that it is business related and that you'd like to schedule some time in the next little bit.

Here's what the email or phone call might look like:

"Hey, Grant. When can I take you for lunch or breakfast in the next few weeks? I want to run a business idea by you to check your interest level."

Simple as that. If they are Champion material, they will be curious and open to schedule some time.

If you get a slight bit of push back with them wanting to know more, here's how you respond:

Grant: *"I'm super busy right now. What do you want to talk about?"*

You: *"I think there's a way for you and me to be doing a bit more business together and want to run by an idea I have for us to Champion each others' business models. We can discuss over lunch to see if it's a fit for us to explore."*

At this point, Grant is either interested or not. If he is, I schedule a time. If he isn't, I put a pin in it.

Your response, if he isn't, is:

"I understand. If that changes at some point, let's grab lunch and discuss it. I'll leave it in your court for now, and you can determine if you want to pick up the conversation at a later time."

And then go on to the next person. In the beginning, I would get the brush off, 70–80% of the time. But as my platform grew along with my reputation for making things happen, it is now 5–10% of the time.

Both are acceptable to me, and it is a numbers game. If 8/10 don't want to have the conversation, it means 2/10 do. And of those 2, if one activates as a Champion and is worth one qualified prospect a month, that's an excellent investment of my time.

And as a side note, after all these years of using this strategy religiously, I also know that 3–4 of the 8 that weren't initially interested, end up coming back to the table and being activated at a later date.

Step 2. Explaining what a Champion is

After the initial small talk that accompanies meeting someone over breakfast or lunch (What have you been up to? Any skiing? How are the kids? What about this weather?), you can get into the meat of the meeting.

Here's the script:

"Grant, thanks for joining me for lunch. I've been thinking for a while that I'd like to be a little more involved with you in a professional way. I like to champion people I like and respect and have them champion me. You are someone I'd like to explore that type of relationship with to see if the fit makes sense for both of us. It's things we would be doing throughout the course of our normal day. And it allows each of us to add value to the other in a balanced and sustainable way. Can I share with you what a Champion is?"

He agrees. *"Yes, tell me about Champions."*

"A Champion is an educated referral source that knows:

1) What you do

2) Why it matters; and

3) Who cares.

Now not all Champions refer prospective clients. Some connect to other professionals that you should know, and that should know you. Some Champions act as sounding boards for ideas — some act as lighthouses to warn about upcoming dangers or of opportunities happening in niche markets.

What's essential for us to being Champions for each other is to understand the markets we are serving, the type of clients we want (and don't want), and current business goals. Then as we start to establish ourselves as Champions for one another, we can figure out what type of Champion we are best suited to be for one another.

The best way to illustrate this is to think of a friend who is crazy about Ford Mustangs. You being his friend doesn't require you to become mad about Mustangs yourself. You are just aware that it's 'his thing.'

So when you hear of a Mustang Car show, you email him to let him know.

When you hear your neighbour is selling the engine out of a Mustang and you know your buddy has been looking for one, you put them together.

You meet your son's college roommate and find out he works in a shop that restores classic Mustangs, you get a business card and pass it along.

If you see an article in the paper saying that there is going to a shortage of aftermarket parts for Mustangs, you might forward that article to him by email.

You aren't going out of your way to do any of this. But when it comes by, you take a minute to let me know about it. It takes hardly any time out of our day but can have a massive impact on each of our businesses. Is that something you'd like to explore with me?"

Grant: *"Yes, I would."*

Step 3. Explain the process of becoming a Champion (education)

Assuming that you have their attention, then we move into explaining what is required to become a Champion. We don't want this to feel like heavy lifting, so we start light. And remember to watch their body language. You are going to get responses from super excited (you can see that they see the potential here), to somewhat interested, to not interested at all. Don't abandon this process if they don't seem super excited. Some people need time to think these things through.

And even if this person isn't a Champion (some people just can't do the function), they likely know people who would be a better fit for you. If they understand what you are trying to do, they will immediately be in a better position to introduce you to others (which, by the way, is them being a Champion of you without knowing it).

But let's look at the script, assuming mild to high interest by the prospective Champion:

"What we would need to do is schedule a lunch. We can get very clear on what the other is working on so that we have it clear in our heads what to be on the lookout for, for each other. I think the best way for me to share information with you is to tell you the three niche markets I'm focused on. I'd share what I do for them, why the solution matters to them, and who is most interested in the solution.

You would do the same for me (we can work on this together) so that I can also keep a constant eye out for you.

Then over time, as I find opportunities/solutions for you that come across my desk and you do the same for me, we can make introductions or bring the others 'attention to it. As well, as part of the learning process, we can give each other feedback to further dial in the types of opportunities we are each looking for. It will be a learning process, and we may not see opportunities every month, but just like the Mustang analogy, you don't see them until you dial into them, and then they are everywhere. I'd be excited to be a great Champion for you."

As you describe the process, watch to see their interest level. Is it getting stronger? Great! Keep going. Are they getting less interested? It might be time to see if objections are forming in their minds.

If interest seems to be waning, say:

"Looks like you have some things popping into your mind? What's coming up for you? Challenges or roadblocks?"

If there are objections, address them as we covered in Chapter 5 and seek to get their agreement to explore this relationship in some format or figure out what would need to be in place to get them engaged.

If they seem engaged and you still want to proceed (use your intuition here), say to them:

"What are some of the business or personal goals you are working on right now? What could I offer in the way of assistance on those goals to expedite them or try to make them easier for you to get to?"

Prepare yourself. Most people have poorly planned out goals, so you may need to work a bit to get this out of them. Remember to always work towards measurable goals. You want a way to measure your activities towards their goals (modelling the behaviour for them to do the same for you). I also like to keep a notebook nearby so I can take notes on what they said to:

1) Ensure I've heard them correctly.

2) Refer to them later as I'm looking to do my first 'pay it forward 'activity for them.

If they say,

> *"I'd like more business."*

You say,

> *"How much more? More revenue (how much?); More clients (How many?) Longer contracts (How long?)"*

If they say,

> *"I need more salespeople."*

You say,

> *"Can you send me your job posting and a description of your ideal candidate so I can keep an eye out? The more information you can give me on*

this the better, so I can work my network a bit and see whom I can introduce you to."

If they say,

"I'm trying to fill up the golf tournament for a charity I'm involved in."

You say,

"When is the event? Where? How many golfers do you want? How many do you have? What have you been doing so far to market it? Who are the ideal people to participate? Do you have materials I can get out into my network? I'll plan to attend and put a foursome in."

You are acting as their Champion so they can see what it looks like. You are putting them first in this process to show your willingness to be a great, proactive supporter of their goals.

This approach is rare.

Everyone wants a favour that they can pay you back on later. You are offering support TODAY, which makes you a valuable unicorn in their market. Most of the value you can bring your Champions is through your network of contacts, which is why we are always collecting and sorting people.

The most connected person wins.

Step 4. Explaining your Current Business Goals

At this point, the hook should be set for many of your prospective Champions. You've outlined the roles, the information that needs to be shared, and what you are looking to do for them immediately. Now is the time for you to offer up what you are looking for. Here's what you might say.

"I'm going to get to work seeing what I can do to move that/those initiative(s) ahead for you. Can I share with you what I have on my plate right now?"

Grant,

"Please do."

You say,

"As I may have shared, we are targeting Female Lawyers this year as a niche market to develop. The sweet spot for us is Senior Associates, who don't know how to make partner and Junior Partners who don't know how to originate business.

So I'm looking to:

• *Meet Senior Associates/Junior Partners at Law Firms.*

- *Give business development talks to Bar Associations.*

- *Talk with Managing Partners at firms about their sales training and retention strategies for Senior Associates/Female lawyers.*

- *Connect with other service providers servicing this niche market.*

I'm also super curious about talking to anyone within the local legal community as well as you keeping an eye out for any new stories or conversations you come across impacting the legal profession."

This 'ask 'isn't just off the cuff. For each Champion you approach, you have an idea on which of your niche markets he/she has influence over or ties into.

You are leveraging their existing connections.

You do this work before the onboarding meeting.

You look polished, professional, and smooth to Champion. The more preparation you do, the less your Champion has to do. And the more likely they are to take on the role. This activation is why we did all the heavy lifting earlier; so they don't have to. It's so easy to Champion us because we have made it easy.

Step 5. Explain the process of becoming a Champion (education)

After your offer of support and explanation of the business goal/model, you are building, it's time to deliver the Call To Action to get this relationship into play and activated.

Here's what you say:

"It seems like this is worth exploring for both of us. Do you agree? (Assuming yes). Let me suggest a course of action we can move towards to continue to explore this.

You send me materials so that I can get to work supporting your initiatives and connect you with the right people within my network.

I may have questions that I'd like to send you (or I can call you) just to make sure I'm showcasing your information the way you want me to and to the right people.

I'll share information on my offering to female lawyers (or whatever niche you are targeting) answering the Three Questions (What we do. Why it matters. And who cares). Then just like the Ford Mustang example, you know what I'm interested in when opportunities come across your desk.

We keep each other apprised on what is happening and any additional information that will help us become great Champions for each other over time. Let's ping into each other at least monthly, but when things are happening, drop each other a note.

Let's focus on the quality of opportunity over quantity. I don't want either of us to feel indentured to one another but instead excited once we see a chance for the other.

This process makes the most sense for us in the beginning. We will have time to get to know how to use this strategy with one another. Would you agree?"

Step 6. Tell them before they agree, you'd like to become their Champion (how and why)

Here's the magic and where we throw a curveball. Be brave. We want to create a feeling in our Champions of 'unpaid debt 'to see how they react. Many people are happy to have someone else pick up the tab, do the heavy lifting, or do their share.

There is a minority that always wants things to be fair, or to be 'ahead 'on the favour game with others. We are going to test to see who we are dealing with here.

Here's what I want you to say, which will put them on their heels a little bit (if they are the right type of person we are looking for):

"I'm thrilled we had this chat, and I'm excited to explore this with you, but I have a condition of us moving forward with this....."

Insert Dramatic Pause...

"I don't want you to champion me until I champion you first. I want you to know how seriously I take this and want to showcase to you how much I appreciate exploring this with you. Let me work on your stuff first, and once we get traction, then you can start to keep an eye out for me. In the meantime, just file my stuff away, and you can review it later. Deal?"

This approach will mess with almost everyone's head. They are so conditioned to ask for favours on credit, that by making it a condition of you paying it forward first, they aren't going to know what to do.

Here's what you are going to see:

About **50%** (the **Resters**) will wait until you do something. These are people that have been burnt in the past. Or that don't like to pick up the bill. Make sure to note how they act. This insight is valuable information for us.

30% (the **Rule Followers**) will read your materials and start noodling what to do for you and checking in with you. They may be open to letting you do the first one, but they have one in the chamber ready to go right away. They are respecting your 'ask, ' but getting prepared to reciprocate as soon as they can.

20% (the **Rule Breakers**) are going to try to fire the first shot and put you in the hot seat. They will want to showcase to you that they can deliver and put the pressure on you to keep the pace. These are our 'unicorns 'and what we want.

The second group is also good, and even the first group can have value IF they reciprocate. But if we were honest, the third group is whom we want. You want to feel pressure to be a remarkable Champion to these people, for fear of losing this person who is an opportunity generating machine for your business model right off the get-go. They will keep you on your toes.

Step 7. Suggest scheduling lunch for three months to review how the first 90 days went

"This has been awesome. I'll get you my materials by the end of the week and look for yours. Let's get started once we have shared all the relevant information and let's pencil in lunch in three months to see how the process has gone, and if we both want to continue.

I'm going to do my best to add value to what you are doing, and I know you will do the same. Very exciting. I'll send a lunch invite for three months, and we can shift it if need be. As well, let's keep in touch regularly if we have questions or when opportunities arise. In the meantime, I'm going to start working to assist you with (whatever they told you they needed help with)."

Note: What's great about setting this lunch date for three months into the future? It acts as a 'reporting structure 'for performance.

If they have done a crappy job as a Champion, they are going to cancel it (or you can). If they have done a great job, and you of them, you will take them out for lunch to celebrate an impressive beginning and look to keep it going.

You may need to update them on any adjustments you have made to your business focus in the meantime, and seek the same from them, so you are both up to date with each others 'needs.

Assuming things are going great, schedule quarterly get–togethers. As time goes on and for those Champions who start strong and then fizzle out, they will miss having the lunches, which might be just enough for them to reactivate themselves in your model. I use these lunches as a weathervane of the relationship. If we are creating value for each other, we get together. If they are failing to perform, I invest my time elsewhere.

But what if they don't want to do it?

Least likely scenario: They pull the chute at some point or even at the end of the meeting unexpectedly.

On infrequent occasions, you'll see a prospective Champion that hits the brakes right at the end of the meeting. Maybe they share with you any of the objections we discussed in Chapter 5, and regardless of you addressing those objections, you can't get them back in the game.

Or maybe they act like they are going to go ahead with it, but you know they aren't.

This situation is okay. 8/10 won't be a fit. And of the 2 that might, only 1 will be. Accept that 80% of the people you talk to may not get it. And for the 20% that do, 50% of them won't activate.

These were my numbers in the beginning, but I didn't have this recipe at that point. I think your numbers will be higher than mine, but even so, 1/10 isn't bad when you consider that one person could bring you at least 12 new clients a year. Kiss the frogs; find the prince/princess.

We don't want to put a square peg in a round hole, and 'no 'almost always means 'not right now 'or 'not under the current circumstances. 'What I like to do when I get this response, assuming that they are open with me that they don't think they would like to come on as a Champion, is to make this simple ask:

"I understand that this isn't right for you right now and appreciate your decision. Given that it doesn't work for you, who do you think I should talk to that might be in a position to explore this type of relationship with me? Does anyone come to mind that has your expertise and experience? And please, if something changes on your side and you want to pick up the conversation, I'd very much welcome that — no expiry on the opportunity. I'd like to explore working more closely with you on something like this. I won't bring it up again with you. It's in your court. If you want to revisit, I'll let you initiate."

And that's that. We close the loop and move on to the thousands of other prospective Champions within our reach. I like to make this ask because the person who says no always knows 3−4 that will say yes. And by them introducing me to those people, they open up the potential of me meeting great Champions AND are championing me just by making the introduction. I always show my appreciation when they connect me with other, more suitable people, whether it be making connections for them, or helping them out with something.

One of my biggest Champions ever was a woman who told me during the Championship talk that she wasn't interested in exploring that type of relationship with me. We laugh about it now, but at the time, she didn't know me well enough and thought I was too brash.

Guess I grew on her.

Chapter 8:

The Proper Feeding and Caring of Champions

It takes 10% of the effort to keep a Champion compared to finding and training a new Champion, so don't take them for granted.

Figuring out the 'science 'of how to manage Champions was very difficult for me. I was looking to balance taking care of them enough to keep them engaged but not so much that it was unsustainable, given my schedule.

Aside from the odd breakfast, lunch, or coffee in person with a Champion, each one should take you about 10 minutes a month to manage. Some a bit more; others a bit less.

In the beginning and at ten Champions, it will take you approximately 2 hours a month.

Twenty-five will take you about 4 hours.

Fifty will take you about 8 hours.

You may think to yourself, 'where the heck am I going to find another 8 hours to do this?'

Answer: You don't have to. You will be swapping about 80% of your business development activities for managing your Champions, once they are activated and producing.

Assume you are putting 4 hours a week into building your business. You are out meeting new people, attending networking events, giving speeches, writing blog posts, doing regular/social media, and other activities.

When you have 10, then 25, then 50 people originating on average of 1 qualified prospect per month, you begin to drop the activities that either don't produce the right opportunities or in the right amounts, or are not giving you a measurable and consistent return on your investment. Champions, in just minutes a month, are bird-dogging opportunities for you 40 hours a week or more. Let's be super generous with the time you might invest in your Champions. Let's say that you spend a half-hour a day while drinking your morning coffee. Even with 10 Champions, it would only take you ten mornings. But you won't do this much because it won't require this much. You are only doing one solid thing for them a month. It could be an introduction, a kind act, or something considerate. Don't overdo it because your pace with your Champions has to be sustainable. If you overdo it in the beginning and then drop off when you have 25 or 50, they will notice. Harder to take away things than to add things. During your first coffee in the morning, you can reach out to a Champion by email, introduce them to someone, share an article they would be interested in, write them an endorsement on LinkedIn, and so on. All the while, they are out there, sniffing out opportunities to send to you. Once you see the power of having Champions, you are going to be encouraged and want to go and add a tonne of them to your network. This is a mistake and why I want you to pace yourself. Yes, it is exciting, but you need to fully understand and appreciate how to take care of the ones you already have.

Lots can happen if you build too fast. You start dropping the ball with them. You forget to touch base once a month. You forget to follow up with them on an opportunity they created. You don't make the email introduction you promised them. They get pissed, then disengaged, and then disappear. This is why we pace ourselves in the beginning — investing time on that first ten to understand how to manage our time and their expectations.

There is nothing more disappointing then to invest all this work in the beginning only to lose them due to preventable mistakes. This was something I experienced many times as I was sorting out the implementation of this business development strategy.

The first three months are crucial to creating a new habit for them.

This is going to be a new idea for almost everyone you talk to. They may be familiar with the idea of being a 'centre of influence 'or a 'referral partner, 'but getting indoctrinated into who your niche markets are and how to introduce you to them, is going to take some consistent training. The first three months are vital in setting these new behaviours. The onus is on you to ensure they are adequately trained, pointed in the right direction, and feeling both honoured, appreciated, and served by you.

When you start a new Champion (after the activation meeting), I want you to diarize 90 days from the day of the meeting itself. This is the point where you will conduct your first assessment of them as a Champion (alone, not with them) to determine if they are likely to be a viable Champion long term.

Additionally, I want you to diarize the one and two-month marks as well, where you will check on those dates that you did something to serve that Champion in that month.

At the commencement of the relationship, you will do something first (paying it forward) but also at the first and second-month marks. By the time you get to the three-month mark, you will have done three things for them. They should have done at least two and hopefully three or four things for you over that same period.

As they provide you with opportunities, you will chase those opportunities down and give them feedback on how the opportunity played out. This back and forth is what we want them to get used to and offers a timely feedback loop on the quality of those opportunities. Which ones fit, which ones were marginal, and which ones didn't fit. More on this in a minute.

This strategy depends on intimacy, so build that relationship through open and regular communications. Don't let them wonder what you are up to; update them.

Give feedback on all Champion activities to dial them in. In the first 90 days, but really through the duration of the relationship, give feedback on all activities your Champions do on your behalf.

- On introductions, they make (prospects or colleagues)

- Feedback they offer as a sounding board

- Bringing your attention to market dynamics that could affect your business

Make sure to acknowledge all and let them know what you are going to do with them.

With introductions to prospective clients:

"I'm meeting with John on (Date)."

"I've met with John and here is how it went."

If you are moving ahead with them, re-enforce why it fits and thank them.

If you aren't moving ahead, share why it didn't fit, thank them, and suggest you reconnect and re-examine if something changes.   This feedback loop is critical for them to source the right opportunities and act as the gatekeeper for you from people that don't make sense.

With introductions to colleagues or contacts:

"I'm meeting with Jenna on (Date)."

"I've met with Jenna and here is how it went and what we talked about."

If there is an outcome to the meeting, identify to the Champion what it was and thank them.

If there wasn't an outcome, let them know if the connection makes sense or if you are looking for something different, thank them, and tell them what other types of people might be a better fit for you to connect with at this time.

When acting as a sounding board.

"Thank you for your insight on that. These were my takeaways."

"Here's how I'm going to begin implementing what you shared into my plan."

"This is what I found particularly useful."

"These are some of the questions I still have to answer."

"I will keep you updated on my progress of implementation."

When offering you insight into market dynamics.

"This is what I'm going to do with the information you shared."

"Do you think I'm missing anything in regards to planning, given this information."

"How closely do I need to watch this information moving forward?"

"Are you tracking what's happening actively, or are you just keeping an eye as things go by?"

"Can I check in with you periodically for updates or to share with you what I'm finding out now that I'm monitoring this as well?"

Notice the collaborative nature of the communications in these sections. I want it to feel like 'you are doing this together 'even though it's your business. The more ownership Champions feel over the outcome, the more they are going to produce for you.

Let them feel like a strong voice in the process and that they are contributing and that it matters.

Above all, those contributions need to be honoured and acknowledged as being very valuable to you, even the ones that don't fit. Because this feedback and discussion calibrate your relationship with the Champion, it will only get better over time. The opposite side of the coin is when you are doing things for your Champions, and they don't update you, ask them how things are going. With you giving updates and feedback, that should model the behaviour for them to do the same for you.

Stay front of mind by at least one touchpoint per month.

For your Champions that may not be in building (business development) mode, or who don't need any particular business support at this time, look to see what you could do that might be unexpectedly kind for them. For some of my more mature Champions, or those that aren't in a hunting position, I may do any of the following:

- Get them a subscription to a golf magazine or something else that they are interested in.

- Pick them up a copy of a book that I think they would like

- Sneak them out for lunch at their favourite spot.

- Bring coffee for them and their team at their office.

- See an article that I think they might be interested in and send it to them.

- Drop them a handwritten note to let them know how much I appreciate them.

- Do something nice for one of their family members.

- Acknowledge a birthday, anniversary, or the anniversary of someone in their life passing on.

- Support something in the community that they are passionate about.

- Send them a photo of something I come across that I think they would appreciate.

Little things have a significant impact. Remember that business used to be like this and we have lost track.

Create intimacy by getting to know them as well as you can (professional and personal interests).

Building on the previous point, get to know them by listening carefully throughout the relationship and tracking what they share.

I like to imagine myself as an FBI profiler when doing this. I want to know as much as I can about family dynamics, where they went to school, hobbies, kids, activities they are involved in, activities their kids are involved in, and so on. The better you know your Champions, the more value you can offer them professionally and personally.

Here are some initial areas of research I want you to figure out about your Champions. (Really, I want you to know these about everyone you do business with, not just Champions. It's an overlooked part of getting to know people as a whole. Knowing who someone is as a person, makes them feel special and deepens that intimacy between you even more.)

- Family unit (spouses, kids, names and ages of all). Where did they meet spouse? How many times married? Kids into any hobbies or have particular interests?

- Where they went to high school, university, and any special designations they got from a training perspective

- Types of previous jobs

- Countries they travelled to and those that they liked and didn't. Where do they vacation?

- What they do in their spare time. Hobbies?

- Are they into sports either as a participant or spectator?

- If as a spectator, what athletes are favourites? If as a participant, at what level and what position

- Favourite foods. Favourite restaurants

- Favourite music

- Favourite movies/television shows/theatrical plays

- Unique things they are into that are not common

- Birthday

- Wedding anniversary

- Type of car they are into (if applicable)

- Health issues/concerns

- How they take their coffee

- Favourite wines/cocktails

- Favourite treats, guilty pleasures, desserts

- Their favourite spa, florist, or other service providers

- Things they want to accomplish. Bucket list items. Goals

- Something interesting about their upbringing, parents, family when they were a kid, etc.

Any other pieces of insight that you can gather in conversation that might position you to do something kind for them. You can track these in your CRM. I manage them in the address book on my Mac/iPhone under their contact in the Notes section.

*Kindness is underrated in business and mostly forgotten. Unexpected kindness is a compelling intimacy builder and, when done for the right reasons, creates a powerful bond. Practice it and see it come back to you ten-fold.

Stay current with their needs.

Whenever you are talking to your Champions, don't assume that everything stays the same or is fine with them. Inquire what's new in their world. What are they working on? Are they struggling with anything? What's keeping them up at night? What can you help with? There shouldn't be anything going on with them that you aren't aware of (unless they are keeping it from you) and the more you know what they need, the more valuable you can become to them. You shouldn't have a Champion on your list where if I asked you what they needed, you couldn't answer me.

These initial ten Champions are your starting line, so make sure you have a finger on the pulse of them at all times. Be selfishly selfless. Make sure you care for your needs and their needs simultaneously.

Be a Servant Leader.

A 'Servant Leader 'is a fascinating term. I define it as someone who does work to showcase what others are expected to do. You roll up your sleeves, take care of things, and model the behaviour for others to follow. The mindset of this type of leader is to 'be in the service of others 'and allows you to do good for others knowing that by doing good, good always finds its way back.

But I have a caveat to that. Too often, I observe people who are servant leaders but who neglect their own needs and end up being resentful of the work they do on behalf of others.

A way to avoid this is to adopt my mantra:

"Everyone gets the time of day from me...once."

We've already discussed how there are people out there who will happily take advantage of your kindness and willingness to be a Champion for them but may have zero intention of returning the favour. That's okay. This will happen on occasion, and it says more about them than it does about you. You will proceed in good faith and model the behaviour, but over time your intuition will tell you what you are dealing with. By just observing people, you can learn a lot about them. But you need to be mindful of this. Don't be the sucker and don't be in one-sided professional relationships, or any relationship for that matter.

When Championing others, do it with the best intention possible, but also be mindful of it being mutually beneficial. If you are seeing that it isn't going to be the case, pull the chute, bow out gracefully, and move on to the next person.

Don't let the failure of others affect the way you approach your role as a Champion or your faith in Champions. And as discussed previously, don't offer your best favour to someone unproven. Instead, do something smaller for them to start so you can see if reciprocation is part of their internal process.

Say 'no 'to opportunities that don't fit and explain why.

Not everything your Champions put in front of you is going to fit. This is part of the process of getting to know each other and your business model. Misfires offer an essential opportunity to explore what the 'ideal 'client is for you and what might be in the grey area for your service/product offering.

Don't shy away from having these conversations. Always do so in a respectful way. The better your Champions understand how to pre-qualify the prospects/opportunities they are presenting you with, the better your time investment becomes. A true Champion wants to produce the right things for you and not put the wrong things on your calendar. They will welcome the feedback, if offered respectfully, and will become even better over time. And it's a two-way street. By providing feedback, you are also inviting feedback on how you are doing for them. Get comfortable with uncomfortable conversations because you both have the best intentions at heart.

Track both their efforts on your behalf and yours on their behalf.

The quickest way to lose a Champion is to take, take, take, and not give back. There will be times where one side is doing more for the other, and then this should flow back the other way. Aside from ensuring you are doing your part, track what they are doing for you as well so that you can see the value that they have created vs your time investment in activating them and championing them. This will give us our Return On Investment measurement.

As well, by doing this regularly, you'll be able to notice what 'trends 'might affect that particular Champion's activity. Maybe they are a bit quieter in the winter because they are travelling. They may be more active in the summer because they are attending more social events. This is all valuable data for you to determine where you can derive value and where you can deliver value. If you can't measure it, you can't manage it.

Report quarterly on what their efforts have done for your business.

Appreciation is one of the main currencies of the Champion ecosphere, aside from reciprocation.

Champions need to see that what they are doing for you is having an impact. This part is almost always neglected when someone gets busy. They 'intend 'to reach out and share wins, but get bogged down with activity until the point where an update seems embarrassingly late.

By touching base with each of your Champions at least once per calendar month, you are given a chance to show them love, and update them on what has been happening in your business.

Remember to report good and bad. But the bad (i.e. an introduction to a person that turned out to be a donkey/didn't show up/ was a waste of your time) is never presented as chastising or making the Champion feel guilty about wasting your time or 'doing their job 'wrong. Instead, you use it as a benchmark for them to use moving forward.

Here's a couple of examples to guide you:

Scenario #1. Champion introduces you to a great connection:

"Thank you so much for introducing me to Daria. We connected, and we are going to explore doing some business together. Thanks to you, I think this could be a key connection for my business model, and I so appreciate you putting the two of us together. A perfect connection."

Scenario #2. Champion introduces you to a train wreck that stands you up the first time, is late for the replacement meeting, and spends the whole session talking about themselves.

"Thank you for introducing me to Max. He wasn't able to make our first meeting, but we rescheduled. Traffic held him up a bit, but when we were finally able to sit down, he was generous with telling me about himself and what he's working on. He seemed like a fascinating guy. He didn't seem that focused on building business right now, so not sure where our relationship will go, but I appreciate you putting the two of us together. I think when he becomes more career-focused, there is some stuff we can explore together. Thanks again for making the introduction."

*What you are doing here is letting the Champion know that the fit wasn't there and that Max didn't show well (hence there is some concern on the Champion's reputation of connecting this donkey with people). As well, you are letting the Champion have some additional information that you need people to be of a particular mindset to be able to explore a relationship with them in the future. From this feedback, the Champion may ask you for additional questions they can ask before making introductions they are unsure about.

Remember that everyone they introduce you to is also a potential Champion, so treat them accordingly.

People that you meet may not be a prospective client, strategic alliance, or another role. Your default sorting pile for new connections is to make them a 'prospective Champion 'if you aren't sure where to sort them.

Follow the same process when getting to know them:

- What they do

- Why it matters

- Who cares

- What niche markets they are in/ have influence over

- What role they could play in your business as a Champion

- What you could do for them (being their Champion).

Collect information off the bat to think through how you could use them/be of use to them. As the relationship unfolds, start to explore the potential of moving them into one of your Champion slots if appropriate.

I like to start this process as I do with any prospective Champion. I offer to do a favour for them and, in turn, will ask them for a favour once my part is complete. I don't bring up the Champion conversation yet. I'm just looking to see how they dole out favours and how they receive them. If I like what

I'm seeing, I 'date 'them a bit more and then initiate the Champion conversation.

Always make your Champion shine. Be a kingmaker, not a king.

A great way to start a conversation with a new contact introduced by a Champion is to ask them how they know the Champion. Then I tell them how I know the Champion and what things I most respect about them. I'm a fan of all my Champions for both selfless and selfish reasons. Selflessly, I like to create opportunities for people that are good at what they do, good people, or people that flourish with a little nudge in the right direction or introduced to the right person. Selfishly, I don't hang with losers. I like to be judged by the company I keep. My time is both valuable and limited. I want to work with and Champion people that get things done.

I collect people who I know are at the top of their game, which inspires me to be better every day. I'm selective about who I spend my time with, and if you are my Champion and I am yours, then I put my credibility on the line for you, happily.

Like the character, Harvey Spector says on the television series, 'Suits,'

"Loyalty is a two–way street. If I'm asking for it from you, then you are getting it from me."

Almost there, friend. Last but not least, your checklist for the next 90 days.

Chapter 9:

Getting Started: Your First 90 Days

Your first 90 days using this strategy are you stretching this new muscle and getting it ready for action. We aren't looking for perfection; we are looking for progression. Just like riding a bike. It will feel a bit wobbly as you get the hang of it, but once it starts to click, you are going to be off. But you must stay committed.

Focus on the recipe, focus on the process, and implement it in the sequential order I've laid out here. No shortcuts and no rushing. If you don't do the pre-work, it will not work. If you don't assess prospective Champions before you engage them, you are going to waste your time and possibly the opportunity.

I'd estimate the first few weeks will be you getting yourself sorted. Niche markets decided. Three

Questions developed. The prospective Champion list will be in place (remember you already did that as part of the homework of this book). By the end of the first month, I want you to have had 5 Champion conversations with prospects. By the end of the second month, I want you to have had 10 new discussions.

At the end of the third month and the 90−day point, I want you to have talked to an additional 20 people. When I have clients work on this tempo, we average 8−12 Champions activated out of the 35 people spoken to. As you would imagine, their closing rate goes up as they get farther into the 90 days. At this first milestone, you will have had the conversation with at least 35 people and will begin to be comfortable with the format of these chats.

As well, your radar will be hyper−focused on what people say and don't say, and if any objections came up (please email me if they do − it's a rarity, and

I want to hear about it). You will start to see how some Champions immediately create opportunities, and others take their time fully understanding your model. You will be championing these people and others, so you'll be a skilled technician on the practice of sourcing opportunities for others. If you find yourself with between 8–12 Champions by the end of the third month, you are winning! If you have more than that, pump the brakes tiger. You have either let too many people in or you are very fortunate and walking a fine line that could tip things in the wrong direction (not showing Champions enough attention). If you have less than 8, consider how many conversations you have had and if you are too picky (be objective with yourself).

The first set of Champions are super important as they are your 'lab' with which to experiment. Include family and friends where appropriate as they are often more forgiving of your missteps, and comfortable giving you direct feedback.

You will also be figuring out how to manage your Champions on an ongoing basis. Looking to fulfill your Champion responsibilities for each of them, introducing them to each other, doing something kind and unexpected, and keeping them in the loop with your successes and challenges.

With just 10 Champions at the end of the first quarter, your business model will start to have noticeable and measurable changes in the way you source qualified prospects. What was initially done by one (you) is now being done by 11 (you plus your 10 Champions). Don't forget the Amish barn raising analogy.

Some of these initial Champions are going to be bringing you more than their share of opportunities. Others might take a bit longer to get the hang of it and figure out their footing. Treat them all well (the high performers even better) and be both pragmatic and optimistic, but always tracking performance over potential.

The performance of each of your Champions will be apparent after activating them and having them engaged for a full three months. I've had Champions that exhausted their value in the first 30 days; I've had others that only warmed up in the last two weeks of their 90-day period and sustained for years. I don't make any judgements until the 90-day mark of them being a Champion. By the end of your first 90 days executing on this strategy, you may have some Champions that you have had activated for two months; others for a few days or weeks. All the while, you are continuing to add to your prospective Champion list. I don't want to go above 10, but any

Champions that do not prove valuable will be swapped out at their 90-day date from activation.

Here are some other quick coaching points I want to make before you get after it and get your Champion strategy ready for implementation.

Not settling.

Don't settle for mediocre Champions. I want you to have great Champions because you deserve it. You are going to be a great Champion for them, and if their performance is below expectations, you are going to get frustrated. It will feel unfair. It won't motivate you, and you will end up resenting them. You don't need them to be perfect at the beginning, but you need to see a trend of them becoming a better and better Champion for you each month. This is not only possible but expected if you are clear with them on what you are looking for and giving them feedback on the opportunities they are creating. When they know better, they can do better. At that 90-day mark, be brutal in your own decision to continue with them or not (not in how you act with them). No matter how connected they are, how excellent their reputation is, or how skilled they are on behalf of others, if they can't perform, drop them. Focus on production, not potential.

Don't make excuses for them.

Don't make excuses about why your Champions aren't working. If you have done the work (the pre-work we discussed earlier in this book) and executed on the plan of identifying, activating, and managing your Champion, all while being a good Champion for them, don't invest time justifying their inactivity. If you have done everything on your end and they are not having a measurable benefit on your business, they get dropped. New baby? Are they moving houses? Kids graduating? On vacation? It shouldn't matter to you. You don't want Champions who mentally check out. If they do, you replace them with others that don't.

The only exception to this rule is a Champion that is sick or caring for someone sick (parent, kid, spouse, etc.). They get a pass and a timeout for as long as they need it, but still, you substitute someone into their space in the meantime. I like people that step up for those they love and have no judgement if they check out to do this.

Hold yourself to a high standard and hold your Champions to standards as well. You may care as a person, but from the viewpoint of this Champion model, you cannot let others' excuses impact your business model.

You don't chastise them or verbally challenge them. You simply move on, replace them, and carry on with your goals. If something changes with that past Champion and they re-engage, be open to it but do not hold your breath. How someone does one thing is how they tend to do all things.

Don't be the weak link in the relationship.

In those first 90 days and moving forward, do NOT be the weak link in the relationship. Over-deliver (but only once as you are getting to know each other and they reciprocate), create opportunities, be supportive, stay connected, keep communications open, introduce Champions to each other, and model the behaviour of a perfect Champion. Those that will be great will observe you, model your activities, and deliver you excellent results. It works if you work it. Doze off and your Champions will doze off. Don't stay in touch, and you give them a reason not to stay engaged and keep you front of mind. Don't put all the time investment in only to watch it fall apart on the little things. Be the Champion you wish you had.

Champions have expiry dates.

All good things must come to an end, and even the best Champion will run their course. Some last a few months; some a decade. Don't be attached to saving the relationship if you are doing what you are supposed to and not getting the same opportunities in return. Don't mourn what 'used to be' and 'isn't any more.' This is why we continue to find new and better Champions to strengthen our business model. As you get better at using this strategy, you will bring in even stronger people. Some of my Champions I have to be careful with. I ask them for a yard, and they try to give me a mile. Because they know if I owe them a favour, I'm going to work very hard to level things back up. I've had to ask Champions to hit the pause button on referrals because I couldn't keep up with the volume they were delivering. What a great challenge to have.

Drafting up.

You should always be looking to improve your team. Your Champions might be great, but they can still be better. Don't become complacent and think, 'it's good enough.' It's never good enough. It can always be better, and you might be one person away from a Champion that originates 20%, 50%, or 80% of your revenue opportunities in the next year. But maybe you don't talk to them because your 'Champion stable' is full. While I want you to hold your initial stable to 10, if you find a monster of a Champion slide them in and drop your 10th weakest Champion — only so many seats on the bus.

On-board openly; off-board passively.

While you are to be intentional on how you bring Champions on board, the inverse is true for off-boarding Champions that aren't performing, underperforming, or who can be replaced by someone better.

Your time is finite, so once you have a full roster of Champions, you stick to that number and just continue to upgrade. Someone that may have been your first Champion and that you were excited about may not even meet your minimums regarding performance, 12 months from now. When they've got to go, they've got to go.

When you find yourself off-boarding a Champion, don't call them and say,

"Listen..you just aren't doing a good enough job. So pound sand... I'm replacing you."

Instead, you just let them die on the vine. You stop your monthly outreach to them. You stop looking to create opportunities for them. The well runs dry over time. If they check in with you and want to re-activate, you can explore that, but in my experience this is rarely the case. Don't try to hold on. Let it die a natural, quiet death as you move on. If they ask why you stopped Championing them, tell them that you noticed things slowed down on their side and assumed they were busy with other things.

Don't lose track of the importance of foundation in the first 90 days.

There are only three objectives to accomplish in the first 90 days. Anything else is moot.

1) You are getting your house in order ready to be championed and preparing to onboard your first 8–10 Champions.

2) You start having the Champion discussion regularly with would-be Champions, practicing first with people you already know very well.

3) Once Champions are activated, you practice being an exceptional Champion, manage these relationships well, and practice giving feedback on opportunities and further clarifying your business model to Champions.

What success looks like at 90 days.

Success will come from having active Champions, knowing how to source them, activate them, and manage them, along with clarity on how to Champion them seamlessly and effortlessly. 10 Champions is a gold medal.

But that's not it. We want to forecast what things will look like as Champions grow. This is all about sustainability and scalability. Sustainability is being able to run it in your sleep. Scalability is, once you understand this model front to back, inside to outside, starting to increase your number of Champions. Here are some guidelines on what to be focused on during which time period.

First six months

- Find, activate, and manage ten quality Champions that are producing (on average) one qualified prospect or opportunity per month.

- Be clear on how you educate people about what you do.

- Be your network's greatest Champion and a model for others.

From six–twelve months

- Resist the urge not to heed my warnings and start loading up your Champion stable. We are building a foundation here. I want you as comfortable as possible before you scale.

- I want you to be clear on how much time it is taking you to manage your Champions. As you get better, it may take less time, but in the beginning, be hyper–aware, you are feeding and caring for them properly.

- I'm aware that you may lose one or two Champions due to mismanagement and need to replace them to bring your number back to ten. Stand before you walk; walk before you run.

- Make sure you are tracking and trending performance. For those that fall off the rails or underperform, due your best to diagnose what the problem is so you can try to avoid it during your recruiting process.

From twelve to eighteen months:

- Move your Champion group from 10 to 25

- Start culling your list a bit as you grow and bring on better people.

- Each Champion should be introducing you to at least one more Champion for you to explore. So ten becomes 20 through internal introductions, and you find an additional five on your own.

- Sit at 25 for a while. This is 25 people you need to Champion and that you need to touch base with at least 1x per calendar month. It seems like a lot but can be done in a few hours a month. Assuming you aren't meeting them in person (only meet your best Champions), all, aside from recruiting, can be done by phone, video, email.

18 months and on.

- Assuming everything is going well, Champions are happy and producing, and you are managing them properly, it's time to move up to 50 Champions (maximum for this strategy).

- Make sure to introduce Champions to one another.

- Assuming each of your 25 Champions introduces you to one more, you are quickly at 50. Some Champions will connect you to multiples, which gives you an excellent pool to draft your best Champions from.

- Managing 50 Champions takes about an hour or two per week — not a bad trade-off when you are getting 50 people bird-dogging opportunities for you.

- Most of your efforts aside from your work responsibilities is to do 'air traffic control' on opportunities and send them to the right Champion(s).

- If you are getting inundated with opportunities from your 50 to a point where you are having a hard time keeping up, ask them to throttle back a bit. Let them know you have lots on your plate and to slow down opportunity/prospect procurement for the short term to let you catch up.

Before I let you go, and to confirm my role as a broken record player.

Do not rush these steps or this process.

This will become a career–long strategy that you can implement, further refine, and reap the rewards for decades to come.

Conclusion

Let's make some money! Most readers abandon books halfway through reading, intending to pick them up down the road. They don't.

Business development, like anything in life, requires foresight, commitment, and patience: the vision to see what can be; the commitment to see things through from beginning to end (even during the challenging parts); and patience to give things time to root and grow. You don't dig up the garden you just planted a week ago to see if the vegetables are growing. You have faith that with the proper steps, watering and watching, you will reap the harvest that you intended. And if you don't, you reverse engineer the steps, see where you went off plan, restart and try harder for a better outcome.

This is where I will leave you. I've sincerely enjoyed writing this book for you to read and use. I always start a book with the excitement of a cat being given a bath. But as I begin to go through and document the processes, my inner sales nerd comes out, and I feel myself sitting here with a smile, happy that I can get these thoughts down on paper for others to use. This strategy is one of my favourites and one I use daily.

For those of you who implement this strategy, I look forward to hearing about your successes. Please drop a line and let me know how it is working for you and if you were able to be patient enough to follow the timeline. I love getting those emails. But promise me this. If you ever think that you have 'built your Champion network and can stop now (because it's on Autopilot), please re-read parts of this book first.

For those that get to the top of the hill and then decide to 'let it ride,' they are almost sure to tumble back down and find themselves with a handful of

Champions (if lucky). Even if it isn't a conscious decision, if you find yourself mismanaging opportunities presented by Champions, not reaching out to them monthly, or not getting back to them right away, I want you to send up a red flag and quickly recalibrate. I have made all of these mistakes. I've found myself at the bottom of the hill only to have to do the climb up to 50 again. The hardest part is knowing that I had my Champion team in place and then taking my eye off the ball burned it all down.

When you find yourself in this place of a small group of Champions and no current prospects for new ones, you'll realize that it's all on you and being in that place sucks.

I'd rather you have a full team and always looking to add bench strength to it. As the years go on, you will become a pro at this and within a few years, you will have 50 of the best trained, most influential, originators for your business. The days are long, but the years are short. Focus, and you'll be there before you know it.

But if, like me, you find yourself having messed up and stumbling down the hill. Just stop. Sometimes we need to rebuild things to be reminded how important they are and because you have done this already, it will be much easier for you. You aren't stalled at 10 or 25 for a certain amount of time. You can make your prospective Champion list, have the conversation, activate them, and go back to reaping the spoils of your efforts. You'll likely have an even stronger professional network afterwards. What I'm trying to convey to you is not to abandon this strategy just because you mess it up (yes, you will likely mess it up). You can always pick up this book, remind yourself of the steps, and get underway.

Discipline equals freedom, so make the building and maintaining of your Champions a weekly affair. Just as you would review your Sales Funnel and Profit Model at the beginning and end of each week, find time to look at your Champion list (or print and post near your workspace) and ensure that these full time, unpaid, opportunity creators are being cared for and championed themselves.

I look forward to hearing from you about how you have implemented this strategy and the successes you are sure to enjoy through your focussed efforts. As always, if I can Champion you, please let me know. Feel free to connect with me online.

Best,

Chris.

About the Author

Christopher Flett, referred to by Business Week magazine, as the Shock Jock of Business Management, has settled down in recent years. His direct, to the point, presentation style is warmly welcomed by entrepreneurial and corporate audiences around the globe. His work has been featured in Entrepreneur Magazine, Fast Company, the New York Times, the Guardian, the Financial Times, the Globe & Mail, CNN, NBC's 'The Today Show', and MSNBC. His previous books include, 'What Men Don't Tell Women About Business – Opening up the Heavily Guarded Alpha Male Playbook' (Wiley, 2007) and 'Market Shark – How to be a BIG FISH in a Small Pond." (Norsemen Books, 2014).

Delivering over 150 keynotes per year, he enjoys engaging with diverse audiences, corporate leadership, entrepreneurs, and community leaders to showcase 'easy to implement 'tools that can have a measurable and sustainable impact on their business model and bottom line'. For more information about having Christopher as a speaker for your organization, association, or event, you can visit: www.ChrisFlett.com

For more information on the Ghost CEO™ Business Coaching model, please visit: www.GhostCEO.com